Invisible Wounds of War

Summary and Recommendations for
Addressing Psychological and Cognitive Injuries

TERRI TANIELIAN, LISA H. JAYCOX, TERRY L. SCHELL, GRANT N. MARSHALL,
M. AUDREY BURNAM, CHRISTINE EIBNER, BENJAMIN R. KARNEY,
LISA S. MEREDITH, JEANNE S. RINGEL, MARY E. VAIANA,
AND THE INVISIBLE WOUNDS STUDY TEAM

Sponsored by the California Community Foundation

Center for Military Health Policy Research

A JOINT ENDEAVOR OF RAND HEALTH AND THE
RAND NATIONAL SECURITY RESEARCH DIVISION

This work was funded by a grant from the Iraq Afghanistan Deployment Impact Fund, which is administered by the California Community Foundation. The study was conducted jointly under the auspices of the Center for Military Health Policy Research, a RAND Health center, and the Forces and Resources Policy Center of the National Security Research Division (NSRD).

Library of Congress Cataloging-in-Publication Data is available for this publication.

ISBN 978-0-8330-4453-2

The RAND Corporation is a nonprofit research organization providing objective analysis and effective solutions that address the challenges facing the public and private sectors around the world. RAND's publications do not necessarily reflect the opinions of its research clients and sponsors.

RAND® is a registered trademark.

Cover design by Eileen Delson La Russo
Cover photo: U.S. Army photo by SPC Eric Jungels

Published 2008 by the RAND Corporation
1776 Main Street, P.O. Box 2138, Santa Monica, CA 90407-2138
1200 South Hayes Street, Arlington, VA 22202-5050
4570 Fifth Avenue, Suite 600, Pittsburgh, PA 15213
RAND URL: http://www.rand.org/
To order RAND documents or to obtain additional information, contact
Distribution Services: Telephone: (310) 451-7002;
Fax: (310) 451-6915; Email: order@rand.org

Preface

Since October 2001, approximately 1.64 million U.S. troops have been deployed for Operations Enduring Freedom and Iraqi Freedom (OEF/OIF) in Afghanistan and Iraq. Early evidence suggests that the psychological toll of these deployments—many involving prolonged exposure to combat-related stress over multiple rotations—may be disproportionately high compared with the physical injuries of combat. Concerns have been most recently centered on two combat-related injuries in particular: post-traumatic stress disorder and traumatic brain injury. Many recent reports have referred to these as the signature wounds of the Afghanistan and Iraq conflicts. With the increasing concern about the incidence of suicide and suicide attempts among returning veterans, concern about depression is also on the rise.

The study discussed in this monograph focuses on post-traumatic stress disorder, major depression, and traumatic brain injury, not only because of current high-level policy interest but also because, unlike the physical wounds of war, these conditions are often invisible to the eye, remaining invisible to other servicemembers, family members, and society in general. All three conditions affect mood, thoughts, and behavior; yet, these wounds often go unrecognized and unacknowledged. The effect of traumatic brain injury is still poorly understood, leaving a large gap in knowledge related to how extensive the problem is or how to address it.

RAND conducted a comprehensive study of the post-deployment health-related needs associated with post-traumatic stress disorder, major depression, and traumatic brain injury among OEF/OIF veterans; the health care system in place to meet those needs; gaps in the care system; and the costs associated with these conditions and providing quality health care to all those in need.

This monograph summarizes key findings and recommendations from a larger RAND document entitled *Invisible Wounds of War: Psychological and Cognitive Injuries, Their Consequences, and Services to Assist Recovery* (Tanielian and Jaycox [Eds.], Santa Monica, Calif.: RAND Corporation, MG-720-CCF, 2008). Readers desiring more details are referred to that document. Both monographs should be of interest to mental health treatment providers; health policymakers, particularly those charged with caring for our nation's veterans; and U.S. service men and women, their families, and the concerned public. All the research products from this study are available at http://veterans.rand.org.

Interviews with senior Office of the Secretary of Defense (OSD) and Service (Army, Navy, Air Force, Marine Corps) staff within the Department of Defense and within the Veterans Health Administration informed our efforts to document the treatment and support programs available to this population. Note, however, that the views expressed in this monograph do not reflect official policy or the position of the U.S. government or any of the institutions we included in our interviews.

This work was funded by a grant from the Iraq Afghanistan Deployment Impact Fund, which is administered by the California Community Foundation. The fund had no role in the design and conduct of this study; collection, management, analysis, or interpretation of data; or preparation of this document. The study was conducted jointly under the auspices of the Center for Military Health Policy Research, a RAND Health center, and the Forces and Resources Policy Center of the National Security Research Division (NSRD). The principal investigators (PIs) are Terri Tanielian and Lisa H. Jaycox. More information about RAND is available at www.rand.org.

Study Directors
Terri Tanielian
Lisa H. Jaycox

Management Team

Terri Tanielian	Lisa S. Meredith
Lisa H. Jaycox	Christine Eibner
M. Audrey Burnam	Jeanne S.Ringel
Terry L. Schell	Karen N. Metscher
Grant N. Marshall	Gail Fisher
Benjamin R. Karney	

Survey Team
Terry L. Schell[a]
Grant N. Marshall[a]
Jeremy N. V. Miles
Gail Fisher
Karen N. Metscher
Lisa H. Jaycox
Terri Tanielian

Economics/Costs
Christine Eibner[a]
Jeanne S. Ringel[a]
Beau Kilmer
Rosalie Liccardo Pacula
Claudia Diaz
Regina A. Shih

Literature Review of Consequences
Benjamin R. Karney[a]
Rajeev Ramchand
Karen Chan Osilla
Leah Calderone-Barnes
Rachel Burns

Systems of Care
M. Audrey Burnam[a]
Lisa S. Meredith[a]
Elizabeth D'Amico
Todd C. Helmus
Robert A. Cox
Laurie T. Martin
Diane C. Schoeff
Rachel Burns
Kayla M. Williams
Michael R. Yochelson
Ellen Burke Beckjord
Andrew M. Parker
Manan M. Trivedi
Sarah Gaillot

Communications Support
Mary E. Vaiana[a]
David M. Adamson
Jerry M. Sollinger

Administrative Support
Samantha Abernethy
Catherine Chao
Taria Francois
Stacy Fitzsimmons
Michael Woodward

[a] Denotes team leader.

Contents

Figures

Acknowledgments

The authors acknowledge several individuals without whom this study and monograph would not be possible. We thank Susan Hosek, James Hosek, Margaret Harrell, Suzanne Wenzel, and Paul Koegel for their guidance and advice throughout this project. We thank LTC David Benedek, Howard Goldman, Cathy Sherbourne, LTG Ronald Blanck (Ret.), Thomas Garthwaite, and Carole Gresenz for their careful review and comments on earlier drafts of the full monograph. We are also indebted to Marian Branch for her editorial assistance.

We thank COL Charles C. Engel and the staff of the Deployment Health Clinical Center for providing us with feedback and inspiration. We are grateful to the many military and veteran service organizations that offered access to their membership and provided valuable feedback on the needs of this population. We are also grateful for the funding support provided by the Iraq Afghanistan Deployment Impact Fund, which is administered by the California Community Foundation.

We acknowledge the many RAND staff who contributed to the successful completion of this work—most notably, Samantha Abernethy and Taria Francois for their able administrative assistance and Diane Schoeff for her coordination of our many data-collection activities. Finally, we thank the men and women of the United States armed forces, particularly those veterans of Operations Enduring Freedom and Iraqi Freedom who participated in this study and who serve our country each day.

CHAPTER ONE

Introduction

Signature Wounds

Since October 2001, approximately 1.64 million U.S. troops have deployed as part of Operation Enduring Freedom (OEF; Afghanistan) and Operation Iraqi Freedom (OIF; Iraq). The pace of the deployments in these current conflicts is unprecedented in the history of the all-volunteer force (Belasco, 2007; Bruner, 2006). Not only is a higher proportion of the armed forces being deployed, but deployments have been longer, redeployment to combat has been common, and breaks between deployments have been infrequent (Hosek, Kavanagh, and Miller, 2006). At the same time, episodes of intense combat notwithstanding, these conflicts have produced casualty rates of killed or wounded that are historically lower than in earlier prolonged conflicts, such as Vietnam and Korea. Advances in both medical technology and body armor mean that more servicemembers are surviving experiences that would have led to death in prior wars (Regan, 2004; Warden, 2006). However, casualties of a different kind—invisible wounds, such as mental health conditions and cognitive impairments resulting from deployment experiences—are just beginning to emerge. Recent reports and increasing media attention have prompted intense scrutiny and examination of these injuries. As a grateful nation seeks ways to help those with injuries recover, research and analysis of the scope of the problem are ongoing, and there is limited evidence to suggest how best to meet the needs of this population.

The majority of servicemembers deployed to Afghanistan and Iraq return home without problems and are able to readjust successfully; however, early studies of those returning from Afghanistan and Iraq suggest that many may be suffering from mental disorders. Upward of 26 percent of returning troops may have mental health conditions, and the frequency of diagnoses in this category is increasing while rates for other medical diagnoses remain constant (Hoge et al., 2004). The most common diagnoses are post-traumatic stress disorder (PTSD), an anxiety disorder that can develop after direct or indirect exposure to a terrifying event or ordeal in which grave physical harm occurred or was threatened; major depression; and generalized anxiety (National Institute of Mental Health, Mental Health Topics page).

Recent data available from the Department of Defense (DoD) (Hoge et al., 2004; Milliken, Auchterlonie, and Hoge, 2007; Smith et al., 2008) provide both pre-deployment and post-deployment data for these conditions. For example, Hoge et al. (2004) examined Army and Marine personnel both before and after deployment, as well as their peers who were not deployed. Results showed that 16 to 17 percent of those returning from Iraq met strict screening criteria for mental health conditions. About 11 percent of servicemembers returning from Afghanistan reported symptoms consistent with a mental health condition, compared with about 9 percent of those not deployed, suggesting that the nature of the exposures in Iraq may be more traumatic (Hoge et al., 2004).

In today's battlefields, the use of improvised explosive devices (IEDs) has made traumatic brain injury (TBI) a major concern for servicemembers. According to the Department of Veterans Affairs (VA), about 1,800 U.S. troops have been maimed by penetrating head wounds and potentially hundreds of thousands more (at least 30 percent of troops engaged in active combat in Afghanistan and Iraq for four months or more) may have suffered a mild TBI as a result of IED blast waves (Glasser, 2007; Hoge et al., 2007; Hoge et al., 2008).

There is some indication that TBI and PTSD have overlapping symptoms. For example, Hoge et al. (2008) suggest that, once PTSD symptoms are taken into account, linkages between a mild TBI and current symptoms or physical health outcomes are no longer significant, except for headache, indicating that some of the experience of such problems may be attributable to PTSD rather than to the injury itself. These high rates of mental health conditions and TBI among post-deployment servicemembers and veterans have led some to refer to PTSD and traumatic brain injury as the "signature wounds" of Operation Enduring Freedom and Operation Iraqi Freedom (Altmire, 2007).

The psychological wounds of war are nothing new. The risk for mental health conditions and the need for mental health services among military servicemembers are greater during wars and conflicts (Milliken, Auchterlonie, and Hoge, 2007; Rosenheck, 1999; and Marlowe, 2001). Combat stress (historically termed soldier's heart, shell shock, or battle fatigue) is a known and accepted consequence of warfare. Although diagnoses such as PTSD were not formally defined and adopted until the 1970s, the existence of psychiatric casualties in war undoubtedly goes back as far as warfare itself (Rosenheck, 1999; Marlowe, 2001).

Scope of This Monograph

In this monograph, we focus on three specific post-deployment conditions: post-traumatic stress disorder, major depression, and traumatic brain injury. These conditions were chosen because of their clear link to servicemember exposures in a combat theater. PTSD is defined by its linkage to exposure to traumatic or life-threatening events, such as combat. Major depression is often linked to grief and loss, which can be salient for servicemembers who lose their comrades. TBI is the result of a service- or combat-related injury to the brain. In addition, PTSD and TBI are among the signature injuries for U.S. troops who served in Afghanistan and Iraq (President's Commission on Care for America's Returning Wounded Warriors, 2007), and concerns about suicide risk make major depression very important to study.

Each of these conditions affects mood, thoughts, and behavior, bringing with it a host of difficulties in addition to the symptoms themselves.[1] Previous research has demonstrated significant impairments in daily lives, as well as linkages with suicide, homelessness, and substance abuse, even when a mental disorder is not diagnosed. Thus, it is important to consider the full spectrum of issues related to how the OEF/OIF veterans are transitioning back into home life and how they will fare in the years to come.

Caring for Invisible Wounds

Rates of PTSD and concerns about mild TBI among those returning from Afghanistan and Iraq have sparked media attention and additional health assessments of servicemembers three to six months after they redeploy. However, the full extent to which mental health problems are being detected and appropriately treated in this population remains unclear. For instance, although the military does screen for post-deployment health issues, health officials have speculated that soldiers leaving the war zone often minimize or fail to disclose mental health symptoms for fear that admitting any problem could delay their return home. And even if risk of a mental health problem is detected among those returning home, whether effective treatment is delivered is uncertain. The Government Accountability Office (GAO) (2006) noted concern about adequate follow-up and treatment, citing low rates of referrals for mental health treatment among those screening positive for post-traumatic stress.

In addition, only a small proportion of those returning from deployment who experience symptoms seeks mental health care, according to early studies (GAO, 2006; Hoge, Auchterlonie, and Milliken, 2006; Milliken, Auchterlonie, and Hoge, 2007). For example, Hoge et al. (2004) found that only 23 to 40 percent of those who met their strict criteria for a mental health problem reported receiving professional help in the past year. Changes in utilization rates of mental health services as a result of current combat operations are also documented. From 2000 to 2004, the number of active duty marines and soldiers accessing mental health care increased from 145.3 to 222.3 per 1,000 (Hoge, Auchterlonie, and Milliken, 2006). All categories of recent combat

---

[1]   For definitions of these conditions, see the Glossary.

veterans show increasing utilization rates, but veterans returning from Iraq are accessing care at a much higher rate than those returning from Afghanistan or those in any other category (Hoge, Auchterlonie, and Milliken, 2006). However, there are still "no systematic studies of mental health care utilization among these veterans after deployment" (Hoge, Auchterlonie, and Milliken, 2006). In addition, although utilization rates for mental health services are increasing, those who are accessing care and those who are identified as needing care are not necessarily the same people.

The federal system of medical care for this population spans the Departments of Defense and Veterans Affairs. OEF/OIF veterans are eligible to receive care through the Department of Defense (while they are on active duty or covered by TRICARE) and the Veterans Health Administration (all OEF/OIF veterans are eligible for five years following military discharge). The Department of Defense does not have a unified mental health program, but a fairly comprehensive array of mental health services is available through the Services, military hospitals, and the TRICARE network, and programs typically are designed and implemented at the local level (Department of Defense Task Force on Mental Health, 2007). As a result, the mental health services provided across the system vary considerably (Department of Defense Task Force on Mental Health, 2007). The DoD mental health providers also collaborate with non-medical support systems, which include Family Support Centers, chaplains, civilian support organizations, and the VA.

Since 1930, the VA has provided primary care, specialized care, and related medical and social support services for veterans of the U.S. military (Department of Veterans Affairs, 2007). The VA operates the largest integrated health care system in the United States. Veterans are eligible to receive care from the VA through a priority system, which is based on the severity of military service–connected disability and financial need. Mental health services are primarily delivered in ambulatory settings—outpatient and community-based clinics, with several specialized programs for PTSD.

The VA has been a leader in promoting quality care in the United States. The VA's National Center for PTSD has been a recognized national leader in conducting research and promoting appropriate treatment for veterans suffering from PTSD. The VA's polytrauma system of care, developed for those with multiple injuries, has rapidly evolved to expand services for TBI among returning veterans as well. However, not all veterans receive their care through the VA.

Over the past year, both DoD and the VA have come under congressional and public scrutiny regarding their capacity to address PTSD and TBI. Congress has directed billions of dollars to address perceived capacity constraints, whether on human resources or financial resources; however, little is known to date about the capacity requirements for addressing the needs of the newest veteran population.

Direct medical costs of treatment are only a fraction of the total costs related to psychological and cognitive injuries. Indirect, long-term individual and societal costs stem from lost productivity, reduced quality of life, homelessness, domestic violence, the strain on families, and suicide. Delivering effective mental health care and restoring veterans to full mental health has the potential to reduce these longer-term costs significantly. Therefore, it is important to consider the direct costs of care in the context of the potentially higher indirect, long-term costs of providing no care or inadequate care. Unfortunately, data on these longer-term costs among the military population are sparse at best and largely unavailable. For this reason, most of the national discussion of resources has focused on direct medical costs to the government.

Increasing numbers of veterans are also seeking care in the private, community sector, outside the formal military and veterans health systems. Yet, we have very little systematic information about the organization and delivery of services for veterans in the nonfederal sector, particularly with respect to access and quality.

Ongoing advances in treatment provide hope for a new generation of servicemembers suffering the psychological effects of warfare. Medical science provides a better understanding than ever before of how to treat the psychological effects of combat. With *evidence-based interventions*, treatments that have been proven to work, "complete remission can be achieved in 30 to 50 percent of cases of PTSD, and partial improvement can be expected with most patients" (Friedman, 2006). Studies continue to raise a "hopeful possibility that PTSD may be reversible if patients can be helped to cope with stresses in their current life" (Friedman, 2004). Similarly, effective treatments for major depression are available and may be appropriate for this population (APA, 2000). However, treatment for traumatic brain injury among combat veterans is still in the early stages of development and evaluation; experts indicate that, with appropriate rehabilitation and treatment, those suffering from TBI can regain functioning.

The Current Policy Context

Public concern over these issues is running high, as reflected in the activity of policy leaders at all levels of government and throughout many government agencies. The Department of Defense, the Department of Veterans Affairs, Congress, and the President have moved to study the issues, quantify the problems, and formulate policy solutions, producing rapid recommendations for changes and expansion of services designed to detect and treat these problems. For instance, immediately following coverage of conditions at Walter Reed Army Medical Center, Defense Secretary Robert Gates formed an Independent Review Group to conduct an Assessment of Outpatient Treatment at Walter Reed Army Medical Center and the National Naval Medical Center. Tasked with identifying critical shortcomings, suggesting opportunities to improve care and quality of life for injured and sick servicemembers, and making recommendations for corrective actions, the group has cited concerns about coordination across the continuum of care for injured servicemembers and recommended the establishment of a center of excellence for TBI and PTSD treatment, research, and training (Independent Review Group, 2007).

Also in the wake of the Walter Reed press coverage, President Bush established the President's Commission on Care for America's Returning Wounded Warriors to review all health care for servicemembers. Its July 2007 report called for radical changes in the disability evaluation and compensation system, but also highlighted the special challenges associated with PTSD and TBI. The report also included a recommendation to authorize immediate lifetime access to care for combat veterans presenting to the VA with symptoms, thus automatically classifying any symptoms of service-connected injury and facilitating access to VA benefits. This recommendation remains under policy consideration as of this writing (early 2008).

In conjunction with the President's commission to look at the military system, President Bush also directed Department of Veterans Affairs Secretary Jim Nicholson to establish an Interagency Task Force on Returning Global War on Terror Heroes. In this task force, solutions were identified within existing funding levels and included a governmentwide action plan. Specific changes for the DoD and VA in response to these groups included joint assignment of disability ratings and co-management for continuity of care.

The work on these issues was also informed by a congressionally mandated DoD Task Force on Mental Health, which operated as a subcommittee of the Defense Health Board to examine matters relating to mental health and the armed forces. Their report, released in May 2007, called for major changes in the culture for psychological health within the military, the provision of additional resources to meet requirements, and enhancements to the provision of the full continuum of excellent care.

The President, Congress, the DoD, and the VA have acted swiftly to pursue implementation of the hundreds of recommendations emerging from the task force and commission reports. As a result, policy changes and funding shifts are already occurring for military and veterans' health care in general and mental health services in particular. Several new programs and expansions of treatment and support services have already been established or are under development. Both the DoD and the VA have taken steps to increase the number of mental health providers; instituted broad-based screening for mental health and cognitive conditions among OEF/OIF veterans within their primary care settings; expanded training in provision of care and screenings for servicemembers, military leaders, and providers; and created new resources for servicemembers and veterans, in the form of hotlines and online resources.

Most recently, the Office of the Secretary of Defense for Health Affairs announced the establishment of the Defense Center of Excellence for Psychological Health and Traumatic Brain Injury. In collaboration with the VA, the Defense Center plans to lead a national collaborative network to advance and disseminate knowledge about psychological health and TBI, enhance clinical and management approaches, and facilitate other vital services to best serve the urgent and enduring needs of servicemembers and veterans' families.

Through these ongoing efforts, the VA, the DoD, and the armed services have attempted to improve the care and support provided to veterans, servicemembers, and their families facing mental health and cognitive challenges as a result of their deployments to Afghanistan and Iraq. To build an evidence base for future quality improvement, a rigorous evaluation of the effect of current and future programs is an essential element of the policy and programming.

Organization of This Monograph

Given the enormous resources being channeled into improving care for servicemembers and veterans who have suffered psychological or cognitive injuries in Afghanistan and Iraq, there will be an ongoing need for information to help influence resource decisions, both for the current conflicts and for the future. RAND's study, conducted between April 2007 and January 2008, was designed to help provide such information.

In the following chapters, we provide the key findings, conclusions, and recommendations from our study. This material draws on a more detailed discussion in *Invisible Wounds of War: Psychological and Cognitive Injuries, Their Consequences, and Services to Assist Recovery* (Tanielian and Jaycox [Eds.], 2008). Both of these monographs and other study products can be found at http://veterans.rand.org. A glossary of key terms used in this summary and a list of references are included as well.

CHAPTER TWO

Study Purpose, Methods, and Key Findings

The Purpose of the RAND Study

Despite the widespread policy interest and a committed response from DoD and the VA, fundamental gaps remain in our knowledge about the mental health needs of U.S. servicemembers returning from deployment to Afghanistan and Iraq, the adequacy of the care system that exists to meet those needs, and how veterans and servicemembers fare in that system. To address this gap and generate objective data to inform policies and programs for meeting these needs, RAND undertook the first comprehensive, independent study of these issues. The study was guided by a series of overarching questions:

- **Prevalence:** What is the scope of mental health and cognitive conditions that troops face when returning from deployment to Afghanistan and Iraq?
- **Costs:** What are the costs of these conditions, including treatment costs and costs stemming from lost productivity and other consequences? What are the costs and potential savings associated with different levels of medical care—including proven, evidence-based care; usual care; and no care?
- **The care system:** What existing programs and services meet the health-related needs of servicemembers and veterans with post-traumatic stress disorder, major depression, or traumatic brain injury? What are the gaps in these programs and services? What steps can be taken to close the gaps?

Methods

To examine these issues, we conducted a series of data-collection and data-analysis activities. We reviewed the existing literature on the prevalence of post-traumatic stress disorder, major depression, and TBI among OEF/OIF veterans. We also fielded a survey of 1,965 servicemembers and veterans to provide data on levels of probable PTSD, major depression, and TBI, as well as on self-reported use of and barriers to health care. We examined the scientific literature on the short-term and long-term consequences associated with psychological and cognitive injuries. We developed a microsimulation model to estimate the individual and societal costs of these conditions in terms of expenditures for treatment and lost productivity. We assessed the systems of care designed to provide treatment for these conditions, evaluated the evidence supporting the services being offered, and identified gaps in access to and quality of care being provided. We supplemented that information by conducting focus groups with military servicemembers and their families and by interviewing key administrators and providers. We integrated our findings to offer recommendations for addressing these gaps and improving quality.

Key Findings

Prevalence of Mental Health Conditions and TBI

- *Most servicemembers return home from war without problems and readjust successfully, but some have significant deployment-related mental health conditions and TBI.*

To examine the prevalence of PTSD, major depression, and TBI among OEF/OIF veterans, we reviewed the first wave of studies that estimate the extent of these problems among servicemembers deployed to Afghanistan and Iraq. More than a dozen studies describe the possible prevalence of PTSD and major depression, but there was very limited information about the extent of cognitive impairments following TBI events. The studies we reviewed and our own data (see Tanielian and Jaycox [Eds.], 2008, Chapters Three and Four) suggest that, although most servicemembers are returning from combat free from any of these conditions, 5 to 15 percent of them may be returning with PTSD, and 2 to 14 percent with major depression. Very little is known about the number who experienced a traumatic brain injury or who are currently suffering from problems related to such an injury. The data are scant at present, and estimates range widely.

Several themes emerge from the currently available literature. Many studies have used common screening tools, facilitating comparisons across studies. But, regardless of the sample, measurement tool, or time of assessment, servicemembers who had been in combat and had been wounded had a heightened risk of having a mental health condition, mostly PTSD. When comparisons are available, servicemembers deployed to Iraq appear to be at higher risk for PTSD than those deployed to Afghanistan. These findings may help to identify which servicemembers will be most at risk for mental health problems upon redeployment, but they offer limited guidance for understanding specific mental health treatment needs among the entire deployed population.

Thus, despite many strengths in the studies reviewed, the studies' limitations call for additional data collection within the post-deployed population.

We identified three important data gaps with respect to generalizability, scope, and availability of information on traumatic brain injury in the existing studies of OEF/OIF veterans:

First, these studies relied on surveys of relatively narrow groups (e.g., combat units, active duty units, Army), making it difficult to generalize findings to all deployed servicemembers, since information about other components and branches of service is weaker or nonexistent. Although the Army has accounted for the majority of the ground forces in OEF/OIF, data that generalize to the entire deployed population would help in planning efforts to address the full array of mental health and cognitive injuries post-deployment across Service branches and components.

Second, very limited research examined associations between deployment experiences and subsequent mental health problems—knowledge that is essential if we wish to understand how we can intervene earlier or mitigate the consequences of combat exposure.

Third, there is limited research on the prevalence of TBI and its long-term effects on functioning.

To address some of the gaps in knowledge in the existing prevalence literature, we conducted a telephone survey of 1,965 servicemembers from 24 geographic areas who had been deployed to Afghanistan or Iraq as part of OEF or OIF. Our survey was designed to capture a wide range of deployed servicemembers across branches of Service, rank, military occupational specialty, and geographic regions. (Details of our survey methods and analysis can be found in the full monograph [Tanielian and Jaycox (Eds.), 2008, Chapter Four].) The following discussion includes data from the survey.

- *Current rates of exposure to combat trauma and mental health conditions among returning veterans are relatively high.*

Rates of exposure to specific types of combat trauma ranged from 5 to 50 percent, with high levels of exposure reported for many traumatic events (see Figure 2.1). Vicariously experienced traumas (e.g., having a friend who was seriously wounded or killed) were the most frequently mentioned. Direct injuries were reported by 10 to 20 percent of the sample. A substantial number of previously deployed personnel are currently affected by PTSD (probable PTSD; 14 percent) and major depression (14 percent),[1] or report having experienced a probable TBI (19 percent). However, it is not

---

[1]   We define *probable PTSD* based on the presence of symptoms in the previous 30 days; *probable depression* is based on the presence of symptoms in the past 14 days.

Figure 2.1
Trauma Exposures Reported by OEF/OIF Servicemembers

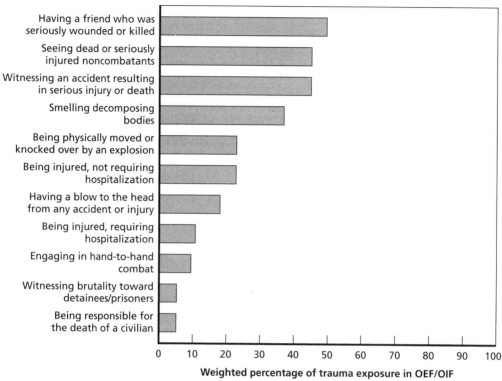

RAND *MG720/1-2.1*

possible to know from the survey the severity of the TBI or whether there is any on-going functional impairment due to the injury.

Assuming that the prevalence found in this study is representative of the 1.64 million individuals who have been deployed to Afghanistan and Iraq to date, we estimate that approximately 300,000 individuals currently suffer from PTSD or major depression and that 320,000 veterans report having experienced a probable TBI during deployment (see Figure 2.2). About one-third (31 percent) of those previously deployed have at least one of these three conditions, and about 5 percent report symptoms consistent with PTSD and major depression, as well as reporting a probable TBI.

- *Some groups are at higher risk for these conditions.*

We identified several groups at increased risk for current PTSD and major depression. Higher rates of PTSD and major depression are found among Army soldiers and marines, and among servicemembers who are not on active duty (e.g., those in the Reserve Component, as well as those who have been discharged or retired from the military). In addition, enlisted personnel, women, and Hispanics are more likely

Figure 2.2
Rates of Probable PTSD, Depression, and TBI

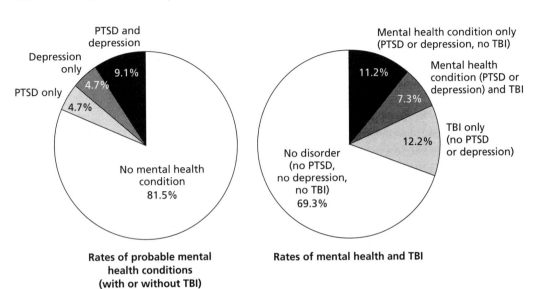

RAND *MG720/1-2.2*

than their counterparts to meet screening criteria for PTSD and major depression. Finally, individuals with more-lengthy deployments (i.e., 12 to 15 months) and more-extensive exposure to combat trauma are at greater risk of suffering from current PTSD and major depression. Exposure to specific combat traumas was the single-best predictor for both PTSD and major depression. Examination of rates of these conditions within the group of veterans who reported no exposure to combat-related situations showed very low rates (2, 3, and 1 percent for probable PTSD, depression, and TBI, respectively). When we used statistical techniques to control for the effects of different trauma exposure, enlisted personnel, women, Reservists/National Guard, Hispanics, and older military servicemembers continued to show an increased risk for mental health problems.

Similarly, we found several groups to be at high risk of reporting a probable TBI, particularly soldiers, marines, enlisted servicemembers, and those with extensive combat exposures. Here again, combat exposure was the best predictor of probable TBI.

- *There is a large gap in care for these disorders: The need for treatment is high, but few receive adequate services.*

Our survey also assessed *use of health care* (seeing a physician or other provider). Servicemembers and veterans with probable PTSD or major depression seek care at about the same rate as the civilian population, and, just as in the civilian population, the majority of afflicted individuals was not receiving treatment. Among those who met diagnostic criteria for PTSD or major depression, only 53 percent had seen a physician or mental health provider to seek help for a mental health problem in the past 12 months. Of those who had a mental disorder and also sought medical care for that problem, just over half received a minimally adequate treatment (see Tanielian and Jaycox [Eds.], 2008, Chapter Four). The gap in care was even higher for TBI: 57 percent of those who reported experiencing a probable TBI were never evaluated by a physician for a brain injury.

Survey respondents identified many barriers that inhibit getting treatment for mental health problems (see Figure 2.3). In general, respondents were concerned that getting treatment would not be kept confidential and would constrain future job assignments and career advancement. About 45 percent were concerned that drug therapies for mental health problems may have unpleasant side effects, and about one-quarter thought that even good mental health care was not very effective. Logistical barriers to mental health treatment, such as time, money, and access, were mentioned less frequently but may still be important barriers for many individuals. At the same time, it is possible that servicemembers and veterans do not seek treatment because they may perceive little or no benefit.

Figure 2.3
Top Five Barriers to Care Reported Among Those with a Possible Need for Services (N=752)

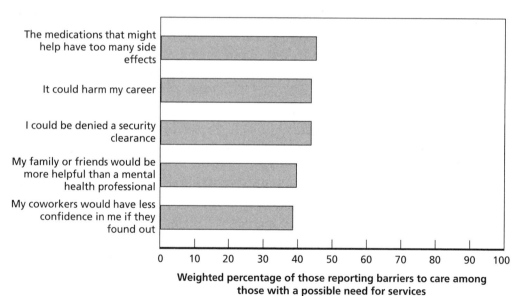

These survey data, combined with the results of our literature review, suggest the following conclusions:

- Most published studies of mental health conditions among military servicemembers and veterans to date have systematically excluded or underrepresented individuals who have separated from a Service or serve in the Reserve Component. Yet, our survey found these individuals to be at significantly higher risk for mental health problems than those currently on active duty. Thus, available data may underestimate the true prevalence of these conditions among those who served in Afghanistan and Iraq.
- Major depression is often not considered a combat injury; however, our data suggest that it is highly associated with combat trauma and warrants closer attention.
- About half of those individuals with a probable diagnosis of PTSD or major depression had sought help from a health professional, but most did not get a *minimally adequate treatment* (defined as [1] taking a prescribed medication as long as the doctor wanted and having at least 4 visits with a doctor or therapist in the past 12 months or [2] having had at least 8 visits with a mental health professional in the past 12 months, with visits averaging at least 30 minutes). Thus, by increasing the rate of effective treatment utilization, we can reduce the number of individuals who otherwise would have persistent PTSD.
- Many of the most commonly identified barriers to getting needed mental health treatment could be reduced if servicemembers had access to confidential treatment.
- Access to both medications and psychotherapies is necessary, since many have concerns about the side effects of medications.

We now consider the potential long-term consequences associated with these injuries.

Long-Term Consequences of Mental Health and Cognitive Conditions

- *PTSD, major depression, and TBI can have long-term, cascading consequences.*

Research conducted in both military and civilian populations on the long-term effects of PTSD, depression, or TBI suggests that, unless treated, each of these conditions has implications that are wide-ranging and negative for those afflicted. Thus, the effects of post-combat mental health and cognitive conditions can be compared to ripples spreading outward on a pond. However, whereas ripples diminish over time, the consequences of mental health conditions may grow more severe, especially if left untreated.

An individual with any one of these conditions is more likely to have other psychiatric problems (e.g., substance use) and to attempt suicide. Those afflicted are also more likely to have higher rates of unhealthy behaviors (e.g., smoking, overeating, unsafe sex); higher rates of physical health problems and mortality; a tendency to miss more days of work and report being less productive while at work; and a greater likelihood of being unemployed. Suffering from these conditions can also impair personal relationships, disrupt marriages, aggravate difficulties with parenting, and cause problems in children that extend the costs of combat experiences across generations. There is also a possible connection between having one these conditions and being homeless (see Tanielian and Jaycox [Eds.], 2008, Chapter Five).

Figure 2.4 presents a framework to help clarify how a mental health or cognitive condition (i.e., impaired cognitive and emotional functioning) has both short-term and long-term effects. The condition can have immediate consequences for the

Figure 2.4
A Model of the Consequences of Post-Deployment Mental Health and Cognitive Conditions

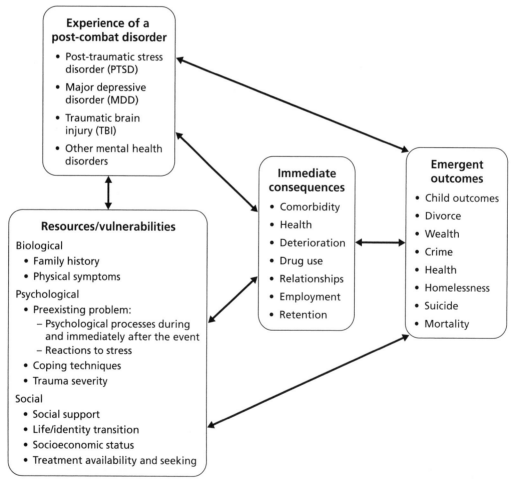

individual (e.g., additional psychiatric problems, poor health-maintenance behaviors), which themselves accumulate and contribute to additional problems (e.g., with physical health, work performance, and interpersonal relationships). The likelihood that the condition will trigger a negative cascade of consequences over time is greater if the initial symptoms of the condition are more severe and the afflicted individual has other sources of vulnerability (e.g., unstable family relationships, low socioeconomic status [SES], a prior history of psychopathology).

The studies we reviewed support this framework. They consistently show that individuals afflicted with one of these conditions experience worse consequences when they must simultaneously confront other sources of stress. In contrast, other sources of strength (e.g., supportive family relationships, high SES, high education) may serve as buffers, even for those whose symptoms are relatively severe.

The extant literature clearly documents that there are long-term negative repercussions of having these conditions if they remain untreated. Thus, efforts to identify and treat these conditions should be made as early as possible. Early interventions are likely to pay long-term dividends in improved outcomes for years to come; so, it is critical to help servicemembers and veterans seek and receive treatment. The literature also clearly indicates that individuals who have more resources (social, financial, educational) fare better; thus, policies that promote resilience by providing such resources could be as effective as programs that target the symptoms of these conditions directly.

Costs

To understand the long-term consequences of these conditions in economic terms, we developed a microsimulation model. Using data from the literature (which had limited information on specific populations and costs), we estimated the costs associated with mental health conditions (PTSD and major depression) for a hypothetical cohort of military personnel deployed to Afghanistan and Iraq. Then, we calculated the costs across the deployed population, based on an approximation for the whole distribution of the deployed population, using publicly available data on the proportion of those returning from deployment, by rank (see Armed Forces Health Surveillance, *Medical Surveillance Monthly Report*).

We defined *costs* in terms of lost productivity, treatment, and suicide attempts and completions, and we estimated costs over a two-year period (see Tanielian and Jaycox [Eds.], 2008, Chapter Six). For each condition, we generated two estimates—one that included the medical costs and the value of lives lost due to suicide, and one that excluded such costs. We were unable to estimate the costs associated with homelessness, domestic violence, family strain, and substance abuse because there are no good data available to create credible dollar figures for these outcomes. If figures for these consequences were available, the costs of having these conditions would be higher. Our estimates represent costs incurred within the first two years after returning home from deployment, so they accrue at different times for different personnel. For servicemembers who returned more than two years ago and have not redeployed, these costs have already been incurred. However, these calculations omit costs for servicemembers who may deploy in the future, and they do not include costs associated with chronic or recurring cases that linger beyond two years. (Details of our model assumptions and parameters can be found in Tanielian and Jaycox [Eds.], 2008, Chapter Six). Below, we briefly summarize the findings from our model, first for PTSD and major depression, then for TBI. All costs for PTSD and depression represent two-year post-deployment costs and are shown in 2007 dollars. Costs for TBI are annual costs based on documented cases of TBI in 2005, inflated to 2007 dollars.

- *Estimates of the cost of a condition for two years post-deployment range from $5,904 to $25,757 per case for major depression and PTSD.*

Our microsimulation model predicts that two-year post-deployment costs to society resulting from PTSD and major depression for 1.64 million deployed servicemembers could range from $4.0 to $6.2 billion, depending on how we account for the costs of lives lost to suicide. For PTSD, average costs per case over two years range from $5,904 to $10,298; for depression, costs range from $15,461 to $25,757; and for PTSD and major depression together, costs range from $12,427 to $16,884.

The majority of the costs were due to lost productivity. Because these numbers do not account for future costs that may be incurred if additional personnel deploy and because they are limited to two years following deployment, they underestimate total future costs to society.

- *Provision of proven (evidence-based) care will save money or pay for itself.*

The costs associated with PTSD and major depression are high, but savings can be attained if evidence-based treatments are provided to a higher percentage of the population suffering from these conditions. Providing evidence-based care to every individual with the condition would increase treatment costs over what is now being provided (a mix of no care, usual care, and evidence-based care), but these costs can be offset over time through increased productivity and a lower incidence of suicide. Relative to the status quo, for which 30 percent of those with PTSD and major depression receive treatment (and 30 percent of this treatment is evidence-based), our microsimulation model predicts that we could save money by increasing the use of evidence-based treatment, particularly when we include the costs of lives lost to suicide in our estimates (see Figure 2.5). For example, by ensuring that 100 percent of those with PTSD or major depression receive evidence-based treatment, we could save $2,306 per person with PTSD, $2,997 per person with PTSD and depression, and $9,240 per person with depression alone (Figure 2.5, left-hand side). When we exclude the cost of lives lost to suicide, evidence-based treatment generates savings for servicemembers

Figure 2.5
Potential Per-Case Cost Savings Associated with Increasing Treatment (Compared with a Status Quo in Which 30 Percent Get Treatment and 30 Percent of Treatment Is Evidence-Based)

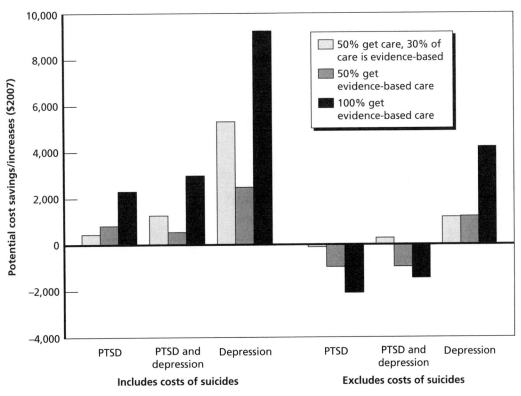

RAND *MG720/1-2.5*

with depression, but not for those with PTSD or co-morbid PTSD and depression (Figure 2.5, right-hand side).

Given that costs of problems related to mental health, such as homelessness, domestic violence, family strain, and substance abuse, are not factored into our economic models and would add substantially to the costs of illness, we may have underestimated the amount saved by providing evidence-based care. However, a caveat is that we did not consider additional implementation and outreach costs (over and above the day-to-day costs of care) that might be incurred if DoD and the VA attempted to expand evidence-based treatment beyond their current capacity.

- *Estimates of the one-year cost of mild TBI range from $27,259 to $32,759 per case; estimates of moderate or severe TBI costs range from $268,902 to $408,519 per case.*

Given the dearth of literature on the costs related to TBI and the effect of treatment on TBI, we conducted a prevalence-based cost-of-illness analysis. Because there is a high level of uncertainty around many of the parameters needed, we develop different assumptions and generate estimates for both a low and high-cost scenario. We estimate that the cost of deployment-related TBI ranged from $96.6 to $144.4 million, based on a total of 609 cases of diagnosed TBI reported in 2005. On a per-case basis, this translates to a range from $158,385 in the low-cost scenario to $236,655 in the high-cost scenario. These costs are applicable to servicemembers who have accessed the health care system and received a diagnosis of TBI; they do not reflect costs for all individuals who have screened positively for probable TBI.

Costs and cost drivers vary substantially by severity of the injury. Annual costs for servicemembers who have accessed the health care system and received a diagnosis of mild TBI range from $27,259 to $32,759 in 2007 dollars. Productivity losses account for 47 to 57 percent of the total costs, whereas treatment accounts for 43 to 53 percent in these estimates. Costs are much higher for moderate to severe cases, with per-case costs ranging from $268,902 to $408,519 in 2007 dollars. In moderate to severe cases, TBI-related death is the largest cost component (70 to 80 percent of total costs); productivity losses account for only 8 to 13 percent, and treatment costs, 7 to 10 percent. Suicide, which we consider separately from TBI-related death, can account for up to 12 percent of total costs.

We estimated the total cost of deployment-related TBI by applying an adjusted per-case cost for 2005 to the total number of TBI cases reported in *Serve, Support, Simplify: The Report of the President's Commission on Care for America's Returning Wounded Warriors* (President's Commission on Care for America's Returning Wounded Warriors, 2007, p. 2). From this calculation, we estimate that one-year costs for diagnosed TBI range between $591 and $910 million. As with the cost estimates for PTSD and major depression, these figures underestimate the total costs that will accrue in the future, both because they are one-year costs and because they do not account for TBI cases that may occur as the conflicts continue.

- *Lost productivity is a key cost driver for major depression, PTSD, and mild TBI.*

To date, other estimates of the costs associated with war have not always included those related to productivity; however, our model demonstrates that reduced productivity is a key cost driver. Thus, future efforts to tally the costs of mental health conditions should consider how the condition affects an individual's productivity (see Tanielian and Jaycox [Eds.], 2008, Chapter Six). Supporting such efforts will require better information about how these conditions affect labor-market outcomes, over both the short term and the long term, particularly for PTSD and TBI, for which current evidence is scant. Additional data on career labor-force transitions (within DoD and from DoD to civilian jobs) and participation could help refine our cost estimates.

Systems of Care

Our cost estimates and review of the literature suggest that providing care to service-members and veterans afflicted with PTSD, major depression, and TBI can help mitigate long-term consequences and offset the costs associated with these conditions. We examined the existing programs to determine whether there were sufficient resources to meet the needs of the afflicted population. We drew on existing documents and descriptions of programs, and interviews with key personnel and administrators of such programs within the Departments of Defense and Veterans Affairs. We included information from focus groups that we conducted with servicemembers to understand their perspective as consumers of these health services. We also drew lessons from the broader general health and mental health services research field to provide a framework for understanding and illuminating both gaps in care and promising approaches for improving access and quality. (For additional details of our analysis, including a summary of the available information on the efficacy and effectiveness of treatments for PTSD, major depression, and TBI, see Tanielian and Jaycox [Eds.], 2008, Chapter Seven.) We integrated information from all these sources to identify gaps in access and quality that must be addressed if the nation is to honor its commitment to provide care and support for service-related injuries and disabilities.

A *gap in access* exists when individuals who need services are not using them. Many factors can contribute to underuse of services. Following a conceptual model commonly used in health services research (Institute of Medicine, 1993), we organize the contributing factors into two broad domains: (1) structural and financial aspects of the health service system, such as eligibility rules, financial incentives, and availability of services, and (2) personal and social factors, such as individual values and beliefs, and military culture (see Figure 2.6).

These factors can be either *barriers*, reducing the probability of service use, or *facilitators*, increasing use. Eliminating gaps in access to care will increase use of services among those who might benefit from the services.

A *gap in quality* exists when the services that individuals typically receive are not consistent with high-quality care. Following the Institute of Medicine's *Quality Chasm* reports (Institute of Medicine, 2001, 2006), we define *high-quality care* as care that is

- based on the best-available evidence and expert consensus about what is most effective
- safe (the expected health benefit is higher than the expected health risk)

Figure 2.6
Health Care Systems Improve Health Outcomes by Facilitating Access to Services That Provide High-Quality Care

RAND *MG720/1-2.6*

- *patient-centered*, meaning that the values and preferences of individuals are respected in clinical decisionmaking, and that patients are fully informed participants in decisions about their treatment
- timely (delays that might be harmful to health are avoided)
- efficient (waste of resources is avoided)
- equitable (does not vary by gender, ethnicity, geographic location, etc.).

Eliminating gaps between high-quality care and care as usually practiced will improve health outcomes among those who use services.

Below, we summarize our findings about the systems of care for post-deployment mental health and cognitive conditions. Since mental health conditions and cognitive problems related to TBI are, for the most part, handled in different systems of care, we consider each in turn.

- *Many mental health services are available for active duty personnel, but gaps and barriers are substantial.*

U.S. military personnel have several options when seeking help for mental health problems, including U.S. military chaplains, mental health practitioners embedded in operational units, counseling offered in community service programs, mental health services provided by Military Treatment Facilities (MTFs) within both specialty mental health and primary care settings. The Department of Defense has also implemented innovations such as collaborative care models (e.g., RESPECT-Mil) that bring mental health services into primary care settings. Additionally, information and counseling are available through Military OneSource, and a range of health and specialty mental health services is also available from TRICARE civilian network providers.

For active duty personnel and retired military with continued TRICARE coverage, efforts to expand the capacity to treat mental health and cognitive problems are under way (including the hiring and training of additional providers), but significant gaps in access and quality of care remain, owing both to structural aspects of the health care system (availability of providers, wait times, etc.) and to personal and cultural factors that may limit care-seeking.

Improving the efficiency and transparency of the system would address gaps in service use. For example, one strategy would be to reconsider policies that limit the scope of practice for military community-service program counselors so that they can provide evidence-based counseling to those afflicted with PTSD and major depression. Expanding training on evidence-based mental health treatments for these providers could aid early-intervention efforts. At the same time, increased reimbursement rates for TRICARE providers could help to increase the availability of civilian providers.

However, even if adequate capacity to provide high-quality mental health services were provided, policies and cultural issues make servicemembers hesitant to seek care. As noted earlier (see Figure 2.3), many individuals in our survey and focus groups reported concern that using mental health services would diminish their employment and military-career prospects. DoD is undertaking major efforts to overcome cultural and attitudinal barriers to getting help for mental health issues (see Tanielian and Jaycox [Eds.], 2008, Chapter Seven), including providing educational efforts aimed at raising awareness among military leaders and embedding mental health professionals into line units. These initiatives can help ensure that servicemembers are aware of the benefits of mental health care, but they do not address concerns about negative career consequences. In addition to educational efforts, institutional barriers, such as the required disclosure of use of mental health services, must be addressed if gaps in access and use are to be closed.

To reduce such barriers, DoD should consider providing access to off-the-record, confidential counseling—"safe" counseling. Providing access to "safe" mental health services would require development of guidelines for command notification; however, the guidelines could be limited and transparent to servicemembers, thereby preserving trust that negative career consequences can be avoided. "Safe" counseling services in garrison could support and supplement mental health providers embedded in units to provide evidence-based psychotherapies for PTSD and major depression and to counsel for a broader range of emotional and situational problems, with confidentiality explicitly ensured and clearly communicated to the servicemember. In addition, it may be possible to harness the powerful buffering effect of social support from peers to help stem or even reverse the development of mental health problems, following recently developed models that engage noncommissioned officers in support of mental health issues in combat zones.

• *Attention to quality of mental health treatment within DoD is needed; the VA offers a promising model.*

Although DoD undertakes significant efforts to monitor quality and consumer satisfaction, it has not developed an infrastructure to routinely measure processes or outcomes of mental health care, and it has not examined the quality of its usual care services. Thus, quality in many sectors of the care system is unknown. At the same time, efforts to train providers in evidence-based practices are under way but have not yet been integrated into larger system redesign for sustainability. The VA, which has focused on performance measurement and quality-of-care improvement for over a decade, can provide a model for DoD, particularly in informing efforts within the newly created Defense Center for Excellence for Psychological Health and Traumatic Brain Injury (see Tanielian and Jaycox [Eds.], 2008, Chapter Seven). Quality monitoring for psychotherapy delivered to military personnel and veterans has been particularly lacking, as it is in the civilian sector, and should be addressed.

• *The VA faces challenges in providing access to mental health care for veterans and deactivated Reserves and Guard.*

Because the VA operates within a fixed budget and uses a priority system to guide access, veterans from different eras are competing for treatment and support programs within a system of limited resources. In addition, younger veterans report that they feel uncomfortable and out of place in VA facilities, in which many patients are much older and have different types of health care issues. This disconnect suggests a need for some VA facilities to make special efforts to accommodate the younger generation of veterans. Geographical dispersion of individuals limits access as well. New approaches to reaching OEF/OIF veterans are likely to involve both marketing and system redesign. Additional data and analyses will be needed to inform capacity requirements, as will understanding the need for services (as might be accomplished with prevalence studies) and types of services offered within each system of care: For example, additional analyses of the number of trained providers available and current utilization at the local level are needed.

In addition, OEF/OIF veterans will need better access to mental health services beyond the VA health care system. Further expansion of *Vet Centers* (VA-run centers that offer benefits and supportive counseling) could broaden access, particularly for veterans in underserved areas. Networks of community-based mental health specialists (available through private, employer-based insurance, including TRICARE) may also provide an important opportunity to build capacity. However, taking advantage of this opportunity will require critical examination of the TRICARE reimbursement rates, which may limit network participation. Determining the best option for expanding services will require additional study. Furthermore, the quality of these services would need to be ensured.

- *The VA is a leader in assessment of health care quality and improvement, but Vet Centers and community providers, including those within TRICARE, still need evaluation.*

A congressionally mandated and independent study of the VA's mental health care services is under way and will be released soon.[2] It is likely to point to areas in which the VA can serve as a model of quality improvement for the DoD and the nation, as well as suggesting areas to target for future quality-improvement efforts. Approaches to assessment include examining administrative and claims data and collecting consumer-satisfaction survey data related to mental health services within the TRICARE network. But performance monitoring among general community providers is difficult. Approaches to ensure quality of services and to inform consumers about beneficial services would be helpful.

- *The science of treating traumatic brain injury is young.*

In the newly emerging field of medical care for combat-related TBI, a key gap is knowledge. Continued research on what treatment and rehabilitation are most effective, as well as on how to identify those in need of care and the level of their impairments, is urgently needed.

- *The difficulty of identifying those with lasting effects from mild TBI hampers care.*

For mild TBI, in which cognitive deficits are less common and more transient (see Tanielian and Jaycox [Eds.], 2008, Chapters One and Seven), gaps in access to services arise from poor documentation of blast exposure and failure to identify individuals with probable TBI, including inconsistent screening practices, personal attitudes and military cultural factors, the overlap of mild-TBI symptoms with acute stress reactions and PTSD symptoms, and possible delayed emergence of symptoms. Materials (e.g., fact sheets, resource guides) developed for more-severe brain injury can misguide or unnecessarily stigmatize or alarm those with mild TBI.

The Defense Veterans Brain Injury Center, now reorganized under the Defense Center of Excellence, is increasing its outreach and training to meet the need for more-

---

[2]   See Department of Veterans Affairs, Office of Policy, Planning, and Preparedness, *Evaluation of Services for Seriously Mentally Ill Patients in the Veterans Health Administration of the Department of Veterans Affairs: Revised Statement of Work*, Washington, D.C., March 2006. This evaluation should fulfill the ongoing requirements of P.L. 103-62, the Government Performance and Results Act of 1993; Title 38, §527, Evaluation and Data Collection; and 38 CFR §1.15, Standards for Program Evaluation.

accurate materials. Strategies to better educate the military community, service providers, and families about mild TBI will complement screening efforts.

- *The complex health care needs of military servicemembers with more-severe injuries require coordination of services.*

Those severely wounded in the war face different kinds of gaps in care. Their injuries typically involve complex needs for treatment, supportive, and rehabilitative services, and these needs change over time. Particularly problematic, and the focus of joint VA and DoD efforts, are transitions from the DoD acute care health system to the specialized Polytrauma Services within the VA health care system.

Work is under way to address these issues. However, principles of patient-centered care and collaborative care could appropriately be applied to the complex needs of TBI patients. Widely applied and evaluated in civilian-sector primary care, these approaches organize care around patients' specific needs and preferences. They are particularly relevant for TBI, for which coordination of care to ensure access to needed services is also critical for more seriously injured personnel.

The VA has announced plans to rapidly hire and expand capacity to provide care coordination, and over the past year the Defense Veterans Brain Injury Center implemented a TBI-specific care coordinator system for those who have been medically evacuated from a war zone. Evaluating the effectiveness of care coordinators will be important. Key challenges to expanding DoD and VA capacity to meet the needs of those with TBI are hiring qualified staff and providing appropriate training in and supervision and oversight of their work. The training of recovery coordinators will be critical, as will training for those providing evaluation, medical, and rehabilitative services.

Strengths and Limitations

Both the strengths and limitations of our study approach should be considered alongside the recommendations stemming from this work.

Our *survey* was conducted independently and was population-based; thus, it provides estimates not previously available, obtained from populations not included in prior reports. Because it was conducted independently of the military and VA, it may contain a smaller potential for bias in reporting than do surveys that are linked to an individual in military records. However, the telephone-survey methodology limited respondents to those with a land-based telephone and those who lived in proximity to a military base. We used standard statistical methods to partially account for these limitations (see Tanielian and Jaycox [Eds.], 2008, Chapter Four). Nevertheless, certain groups are underrepresented in our sample, and thus the overall results may not be accurately generalizable to the entire deployed population.

Our *estimation of costs* for PTSD and major depression was based on a state-of-the-art microsimulation model, adding valuable information to other cost estimates. However, scant research was available for some cost-estimate parameters associated with mental health conditions, and we were unable to use the modeling approach for TBI because of the absence of relevant research. These cost estimates are unavoidably imprecise, due to uncertainty in estimates of prevalence rates, individuals' willingness to seek care, treatment efficacy, the effect of mental health conditions on productivity, and other estimates used to parameterize our model. Nevertheless, all of the parameters used in our model are grounded on prior literature, and we have done our best to be conservative in generating the cost predictions.

Finally, our *review of the programs* now available to OEF/OIF veterans applied a health services model, bringing to bear a focus on access and quality that has been missing from examinations of these systems of care. In our analyses, we focused on three specific mental health and cognitive conditions that affect servicemembers and veterans post-deployment, the costs associated with addressing those conditions, and the services available post-deployment to assist in recovery. The delivery of post-deployment services is part of a larger continuum of ensuring the health of servicemembers, which includes pre-deployment screenings, education, and trainings about the potential effects of combat and deployment. It was beyond the scope of this study to fully assess the adequacy of pre-deployment screenings and training/education programs. However, these programs do require more in-depth analyses to determine their effectiveness. Our findings offer guidance at the system level for improving post-deployment services for those in need following deployment, regardless of the individual's pre-deployment experiences. We also did not comprehensively examine issues around determination of service-related injuries or disability determination, both of which are critical for determining eligibility for care within the VA. Finally, we relied solely upon publicly available information because requests for official data were still under review at the time of this writing.

CHAPTER THREE

Conclusions and Recommendations

Safeguarding mental health is an integral part of the national responsibility to recruit, prepare, and sustain a military force and to address service-connected injuries and disabilities. Safeguarding mental health is also critical for compensating and honoring those who have served the nation. The Departments of Defense and Veterans Affairs are primarily responsible for these critical tasks; however, other federal agencies (e.g., the Department of Labor) and states also play important roles in ensuring that the military population is not only ready as a national asset but valued as a national priority.[1]

While the United States is still involved in military operations in Afghanistan and Iraq, psychological and cognitive injuries among those deployed in support of Operations Enduring Freedom and Iraqi Freedom are of growing concern. Most servicemembers return from deployment without problems and successfully readjust to ongoing military employment or work in civilian settings. But others return with mental health conditions such as post-traumatic stress disorder or major depression, and some have suffered a traumatic brain injury, such as a concussion, leaving a portion of sufferers with cognitive impairments.

Despite widespread policy interest and a firm commitment from the Departments of Defense and Veterans Affairs to address these injuries, fundamental gaps remain in our knowledge about the mental health and cognitive needs of U.S. servicemembers returning from Afghanistan and Iraq, the adequacy of the care system available to meet those needs, the experience of servicemembers who are in need of treatment, and factors related to whether and how injured servicemembers and veterans seek care.

---

[1] In March 2007, the President not only tasked the Secretaries of Defense and Veterans Affairs with making improvements that would respond to stories of systemic failures in caring for the wounded, he also created an interagency task force that also included the Secretaries of Labor, Health and Human Services, Housing and Urban Development, and Education, the Director of the Office of Management and Budget, and the Administrator of the Small Business Administration at a minimum ("Executive Order Establishing Task Force; Executive Order 13426—Establishing a Commission on Care for America's Returning Wounded Warriors and a Task Force on Returning Global War on Terror Heroes," *Federal Register*, March 8, 2007, Appendix A). Indeed, the obligation for care of veterans does not stop at the federal level. Each of the states has a division of veterans' affairs, and since the inception of the Global War on Terror, several states have expanded health care access, education benefits, and job support programs (see the National Governors Association Web site).

RAND undertook this comprehensive study to address these gaps and make these conditions and their consequences visible.

We focused on three major conditions—post-traumatic stress disorder, major depression, and traumatic brain injury—because there are obvious mechanisms that link each of these conditions to specific experiences in war. Unfortunately, these conditions are often invisible to the eye. Unlike physical wounds of war that maim or disfigure, these conditions remain invisible to other servicemembers, family members, and society in general. All three conditions affect mood, thoughts, and behavior, yet these conditions often go unrecognized or unacknowledged. In addition, the effects of traumatic brain injury are still poorly understood, leaving a substantial gap in knowledge about the extent of the problem or effective treatment.

In the discussion below, we summarize our main study conclusions in the three domains represented in our overarching questions: the prevalence of these conditions among OEF/OIF veterans; the costs in terms of short- and long-term health and social consequences, as well as economic costs; and services to assist recovery. We then describe policy recommendations that are based on our research.

Prevalence

What is the scope of mental health and cognitive issues faced by OEF/OIF troops returning from deployment? Most of the 1.64 million military servicemembers who have deployed in support of OIF/OEF will return from war without problems and readjust successfully, but many have and will return with significant mental health conditions. Among OEF/OIF veterans, rates of PTSD, major depression, and probable TBI are relatively high. A telephone study of 1,965 previously deployed individuals sampled from 24 geographic areas found substantial rates of mental health problems in the past 30 days, with 14 percent screening positive for PTSD and 14 percent screening positive for major depression. A similar number, 19 percent, reported a probable TBI during deployment (e.g., a concussion). Major depression is often not considered a combat-related injury; however, our analyses suggest that it is highly associated with combat exposure and should be considered on the spectrum of post-deployment mental health consequences. Although a substantial proportion of respondents had reported a TBI, it is not possible to know from the survey the severity of the injury or whether the injury caused functional impairment.

Assuming that the prevalence found in this study is representative of the 1.64 million servicemembers who have been deployed for OEF/OIF as of October 2007, we estimate that approximately 300,000 individuals currently suffer from PTSD or major depression, and 320,000 individuals reported experiencing a probable TBI during deployment. About one-third of those previously deployed have at least one of these three conditions, and about 5 percent report symptoms of all three. Some specific groups, previously understudied—including those in the Reserve Components and those who have left military service—may be at higher risk of suffering from these conditions.

Seeking and receiving treatment. Of those reporting a probable TBI, 57 percent had not been evaluated by a physician for brain injury. Military servicemembers with probable PTSD or major depression seek care at about the same rate as the civilian population, and, just as in the civilian population, most afflicted individuals were not receiving treatment. About half (53 percent) of those who met the criteria for PTSD or major depression in the past 30 days had sought help from a physician or mental health provider for a mental health problem in the past year.

Getting quality care. Even when individuals receive care, too few receive quality care. Of those who have a mental disorder and also sought medical care for that problem, just over half received a minimally adequate treatment. We expect that the number who received *quality care* (i.e., a treatment that has been demonstrated to be effective) would be even smaller. Focused efforts are needed to significantly improve both accessibility to care and quality of care for these groups. The prevalence of PTSD and major depression will likely remain high unless greater efforts are made to enhance systems of care for these individuals.

Survey respondents identified many barriers that inhibit getting treatment for their mental health problems. In general, respondents were concerned that treatment would not be kept confidential and would constrain future job assignments and military-career advancement. Respondents were also concerned that drug therapies for mental health problems may have unpleasant side effects. These barriers suggest the need for increased access to confidential treatment, including evidence-based psychotherapy to maintain high levels of readiness and functioning among previously deployed servicemembers and veterans.

Costs

What are the costs of these mental health and cognitive conditions to the individual and to society? Unless treated, each of these conditions has wide-ranging and negative implications for those afflicted. We considered a wide array of consequences that affect work, family, and social functioning, and we considered co-occurring problems, such as substance abuse, homelessness, and suicide.

The presence of any one of these conditions can impair future health, work productivity, and family and social relationships. Individuals afflicted with any of these conditions are more likely to have other psychiatric diagnoses (e.g., substance use) and are at increased risk for attempting suicide. They have higher rates of unhealthy behaviors (e.g., smoking, overeating, unsafe sex) and higher rates of physical health problems and mortality. They tend to miss more days of work or report being less productive.

There is also a possible connection between having one of these conditions and being homeless.

Suffering from these conditions can impair relationships, disrupt marriages, aggravate the difficulties of parenting, and cause problems in children, thus extending the consequences of combat experiences across generations.

Associated costs. In dollar terms, the costs associated with mental health and cognitive conditions stemming from the conflicts in Afghanistan and Iraq are substantial. We estimated costs using two separate methodologies—for PTSD and major depression, we used a microsimulation model to project two-year costs. Because there were insufficient data to simulate two-year cost projections for TBI, we estimated annual costs for TBI using a standard cost-of-illness approach. On a per-case basis, PTSD-related costs incurred within the first two years after servicemembers return home are approximately $5,904 to $10,298, depending on whether we include the cost of lives lost to suicide. Two-year costs associated with major depression are approximately $15,461 to $25,757, and costs associated with having PTSD and major depression are approximately $12,427 to $16,884. Annual costs for servicemembers who have accessed the health care system and received a diagnosis of traumatic brain injury are even higher, ranging from $27,259 to $32,759 for mild cases and from $268,902 to $408,519 for moderate or severe cases. However, our cost figures omit current as well as potential later costs stemming from substance abuse, domestic violence, homelessness, family strain, and several other factors, thus understating the true costs associated with deployment-related cognitive and mental health conditions.

Translating these cost estimates into a total-dollar figure is confounded by uncertainty about the total number of cases in a given year, by the little information that is available about the severity of these cases, and by the extent to which the three conditions co-occur. Given these caveats, we used our microsimulation model to predict two-year costs for the entire 1.6 million troops who have ever been deployed. We estimate that PTSD-related and major depression–related costs could range from $4.0 to $6.2 billion over two years. Applying the costs per case for TBI to the total number of diagnosed TBI cases identified as of June 2007 (2,726), we estimate that total costs incurred within the first year after diagnosis could range from $591 million to $910 million. To the extent that additional troops deploy and more TBI cases occur in the coming months and years, total costs will rise. Because these calculations include costs for servicemembers who returned from deployment starting as early as 2001, many of these costs (for PTSD, depression, and TBI) have already been incurred. However, if servicemembers continue to be deployed in the future, rates of detection of TBI among servicemembers increase, or there are costs associated with chronic or recurring cases that linger beyond two years, the total expected costs associated with these conditions will increase beyond the range.

Lost productivity. Our findings also indicate that lost productivity is a key cost driver for major depression and PTSD. Approximately 55 to 95 percent of total costs can be attributed to reduced productivity; for mild TBI, productivity losses may account for 47 to 55 percent of total costs. Because severe TBI can lead to death, mortality is the largest component of cost for moderate to severe TBI, accounting for 70 to 80 percent of total costs. Cost studies that do not account for reduced productivity may significantly understate the true costs of the conflicts in Afghanistan and Iraq.

Evidence-based treatment. Certain treatments have been shown to be effective for both PTSD and major depression, but these evidence-based treatments are not yet available in all treatment settings. We estimate that evidence-based treatment for PTSD and major depression would pay for itself within two years, even without considering costs related to substance abuse, homelessness, family strain, and other indirect consequences of mental health conditions. Evidence-based care for PTSD and major depression could save as much as $1.7 billion, or $1,063 per returning veteran; the savings come from increases in productivity, as well as from reductions in the expected number of suicides.

Given these numbers, investments in evidence-based treatment would make sense from DoD's perspective, not only because of higher remission and recovery rates but also because such treatment would increase the productivity of servicemembers. The benefits to DoD in retention and increased productivity would outweigh the higher costs of providing evidence-based care. These benefits would probably be higher had we been able to capture the full spectrum of costs associated with mental health conditions. Our estimates do not include additional implementation and outreach that might be incurred if DoD and the VA attempted to expand evidence-based treatment beyond current capacity.

Cost studies that do not account for reduced productivity may significantly understate the true costs of the conflicts in Afghanistan and Iraq. Currently, information is limited on how mental health conditions affect career outcomes within DoD. Given the strong association between mental health status and productivity found in civilian studies, research that explores how the mental health status of active duty personnel affects career outcomes would be valuable. Ideally, studies would consider how mental health conditions influence job performance, promotion within DoD, and transitions from DoD into the civilian labor force (as well as productivity after transition).

Systems of Care

What existing programs and services meet the health-related needs of servicemembers with PTSD or major depression; what are the gaps in the programs and services; what steps can be taken to close the gaps? To achieve the cost savings outlined above, servicemembers suffering from PTSD and major depression must be identified as early as possible and be provided with evidence-based treatment. The capacity of DoD and the VA to provide mental health services has been increased substantially, but significant gaps in access and quality remain.

A gap between need and use. Particularly for the active duty population, there is a large gap between the need for mental health services and the use of such services—a pattern that appears to stem from structural aspects of services (wait times, availability of providers) as well as from personal and cultural factors. Institutional and cultural barriers to mental health care are substantial—and not easily surmounted. Addressing the personal attitudes of servicemembers about use of mental health services is important, but it not likely to be sufficient if institutional barriers remain.

Quality-of-care gaps. We also identified gaps in the organizational tools and incentives that would support the delivery of high-quality mental health care to the active duty population and to retired military who use TRICARE, DoD's health insurance plan. In the absence of such organizational supports, it is not possible to provide oversight to ensure high-quality care, which includes ensuring both that the treatment provided is evidence-based and that it is patient-centered, timely, and efficient. DoD has initiated training in evidence-based practices for providers, but these efforts have not yet been integrated into a larger system redesign that values and provides incentives for quality of care. The newly created Defense Center of Excellence for Psychological Health and Traumatic Brain Injury, housed within the DoD, represents a historic opportunity to prioritize a system-level focus on monitoring and improving quality of care. Continued funding and appropriate regulatory authority will be important to sustain this focus over time.

The VA provides a promising quality-improvement model for DoD. However, the VA too faces challenges in providing access to OEF/OIF veterans, many of whom have difficulty securing appointments, particularly in facilities that have been resourced primarily to meet the demands of older veterans. Better projections of the amount and type of demand among the newer veterans are needed to ensure that the VA has the appropriate resources to meet the potential demand. New approaches to outreach could make facilities more acceptable to OEF/OIF veterans.

Going beyond DoD and the VA. Improving access to mental health services for OEF/OIF veterans will require reaching beyond the DoD and VA health care systems. Given the diversity and the geographic dispersal of these veterans, other options for providing health services must be considered, including Vet Centers, nonmedical centers that offer supportive counseling and other services to veterans, and other community-based providers. Vet Centers already play a critical role; expanding Centers could broaden access, particularly for veterans in underserved areas. Networks of community-based mental health specialists (available through private, employer-based insurance, including TRICARE) could also provide capacity. However, taking advantage of this opportunity will require a critical examination of the TRICARE reimbursement rates, which may limit network participation.

Although Vet Centers and other community-based providers offer the potential for expanded access to mental health services, ways to monitor performance and quality among these providers will be essential to ensuring quality care. Although ongoing training for providers is being made broadly available, it is not supported with a level of supervision that will result in high-quality care. Systems for supporting delivery of high-quality care (information systems, performance feedback) are currently lacking in these sectors. Commercial managed health care organizations have some existing approaches and tools to monitor quality that may be of value and utility, but many of the grassroots efforts currently emerging to serve OEF/OIF veterans do not.

What existing programs and services meet the health-related needs of those with traumatic brain injuries; what are the gaps in care; and what steps can be taken to close them? The medical science for treating traumatic brain injury is in its infancy. Research is urgently needed to develop effective screening tools that are both valid and sensitive, as well as to document what treatment and rehabilitation will be most effective.

For mild TBI, a head injury that may or may not result in symptoms and long-term neurocognitive deficits, we found gaps in access to services stemming from poor documentation of blast exposures and failure to identify individuals with probable TBI. These gaps not only hamper provision of acute care but may also place individuals at risk of additional blast exposures.

Servicemembers with more-severe injuries, including moderate and severe TBI, face a different kind of access gap: lack of coordination across a continuum of care. A severely injured individual's need for treatment, as well as for supportive and rehabilitative services, will change over time and involve multiple transitions across systems. Task forces, commissions, and review groups have already identified multiple challenges arising from these complexities; these challenges remain the focus of improvement activities in both DoD and the VA.

Recommendations

Current concern about the invisible wounds of war is increasing, and many efforts to identify and treat those wounds are already under way. Our data show that these mental health and cognitive conditions are widespread; in a cohort of otherwise healthy, young individuals, they represent the primary type of morbidity or illness for this population in the coming years. What is most worrisome is that these problems are not yet fully understood, particularly TBI, and systems of care are not yet fully available to assist recovery for any of the three conditions. Thus, the invisible wounds of war require special attention and high priority. An exceptional effort will be required to ensure that they are appropriately recognized and treated.

Looking across the dimensions of our analysis, and in light of the strengths and limitations of our methodology, we offer four specific recommendations that we believe would improve the understanding and treatment of PTSD, major depression, and TBI among military veterans. We briefly describe each recommendation, and then discuss some of the issues that would need to be addressed for successful implementation. We believe efforts to address these recommendations should be standardized to the greatest extent possible *within DoD* (across Service branches, with appropriate guidance from the Assistant Secretary of Defense for Health Affairs), *within the VA* (across health care facilities and Vet Centers), and *across these systems* and extended *into the community-based civilian sector.*

1. **Increase the cadre of providers who are trained and certified to deliver proven (evidence-based) care, so that capacity is adequate for current and future needs.**

There is substantial unmet need for treatment of PTSD and major depression among military servicemembers following deployment. Both DoD and the VA have had difficulty recruiting and retaining appropriately trained mental health profession-als to fill existing *or* new slots. With the possibility of more than 300,000 new cases of mental health conditions among OEF/OIF veterans, a commensurate increase in treat-ment capacity is needed. Increased numbers of trained and certified professionals are needed to provide high-quality care in all sectors, both military and civilian, serving previously deployed personnel. Although the precise increase of newly trained provid-ers is not yet known, it is likely to number in the thousands. These would include pro-viders not just in specialty mental health settings, but also those embedded in settings such as primary care, where servicemembers already are served. Stakeholders consis-tently referred to challenges in hiring and retaining trained mental health providers. Determining the exact number of providers will require further analyses of demand projections over time that take into account the expected length of evidence-based treatment and desired utilization rates.

Additional training in evidence-based approaches for trauma will also be required for tens of thousands of existing providers. Moreover, since there is already an increased need for services, the required expansion in trained providers is already several years overdue.

This large-scale training effort necessitates substantial investment immediately. Such investment could be facilitated by several strategies, including

- development of a certification process to document the qualifications of provid-ers. Rather than rely on a system in which any licensed counselor is assumed to have all necessary skills regardless of training, certification should confirm that a provider is trained to use specific evidence-based treatment for specific conditions. Providers would also be required to demonstrate requisite knowledge of unique military culture, military employment, and issues relevant to veterans (gained through their prior training and through the new training/certification we are recommending).

- adjustment of financial reimbursement for providers to offer appropriate compensation and incentives to attract and retain highly qualified professionals and ensure motivation for delivering quality care.
- expansion of existing training programs for psychiatrists, psychologists, social workers, marriage and family therapists, and other counselors. Programs should include training in specific therapies related to trauma and to military culture.
- establishment of regional training centers for joint training of DoD, VA, and civilian providers in evidence-based care for PTSD and major depression. The centers should be federally funded, possibly outside of DoD and VA budgets. This training could occur in coordination with or through the Department of Health and Human Services. Training should be standardized across training centers to ensure both consistency and increased fidelity in treatment delivery.
- linkage of certification to training to ensure that providers not only receive required training but also are supervised and monitored to verify that quality standards are met and maintained over time.
- retraining or expansion of existing providers within DoD and the VA (e.g., military community-service program counselors) to include delivery or support of evidence-based care.
- evaluation of training efforts as they are rolled out, so that we understand how much training is needed and of what type, thereby ensuring delivery of effective care.

2. Change policies to encourage active duty personnel and veterans to seek needed care.

Creating an adequate supply of well-trained professionals to provide care is but one facet of ensuring access to care. Strategies must also increase demand for necessary services. Many servicemembers are reluctant to seek services for fear of negative career repercussions. Policies must be changed so that there are no perceived or real adverse career consequences for individuals who seek treatment, except when functional impairment (e.g., poor job performance or being a hazard to oneself or others) compromises fitness for duty. Primarily, such policies will require creating new ways for servicemembers and veterans to obtain treatments that are confidential, to operate in parallel with existing mechanisms for receiving treatment (e.g., command referral, unit-embedded support, or self-referral).

We are not suggesting that the confidentiality of treatment should be absolute; both military and civilian treatment providers already have a legal obligation to report to authorities or commanders any patients that represent a threat to themselves or others. However, information about being in treatment is currently available to command staff, although treatment itself is not a sign of dysfunction or poor job performance and may not have any relationship to deployment eligibility. Providing an option for confidential treatment has the potential to increase total-force readiness by encouraging individuals to seek needed health care before problems accrue to a critical level. In this way, mental health treatment would be appropriately used by the military as a tool to avoid or mitigate functional impairment, rather than as evidence of functional impairment. We believe this would ultimately lead to better force readiness and retention, thus being a beneficial change both for the organization and for the individual.

This recommendation would require resolving many practical challenges, but it is vital for addressing the mental health problems of those servicemembers who are not seeking care because they are concerned for their military careers.

Specific strategies for facilitating care-seeking include the following:

- Develop strategies for early identification of problems that can be confidential, so that problems are recognized and care sought early, before problems lead to impairments in daily life, including job function or eligibility for deployment.
- Develop ways for servicemembers to seek mental health care voluntarily and off-the-record, including ways to allow servicemembers to seek this care off-base if they prefer and ways to pay for confidential mental health care (that is, not necessarily tied to an insurance claim from the individual servicemember). Thus, the care would be offered to military personnel without mandating disclosure, unless the servicemember chooses to disclose use of mental health care or there is a command-initiated referral to mental health care.
- Separate the system for determining deployment eligibility from the mental health care system. This may require the development of new ways to determine fitness for duty and eligibility for deployment that do not include information about mental health service use.
- Make the system transparent to servicemembers so that they understand how information about mental health services is and is not used. Such transparency may help mitigate servicemembers' concerns about a detriment to their careers.

3. Deliver proven, evidence-based care to servicemembers and veterans whenever and wherever services are provided.

Our extensive review of the scientific literature documented that treatments for PTSD and major depression vary substantially in their effectiveness. In addition, the recent report from the Institute of Medicine (2007) shows reasonable evidence for treatments for PTSD among military servicemembers and veterans. Our evaluation shows that the most effective treatments are being delivered in some sectors of the care system for military personnel and veterans, but that gaps remain in systemwide implementation. Delivery of evidence-based care to all veterans with PTSD or major depression would pay for itself, or even save money, by improving productivity and reducing medical and mortality costs within only two years. Providing evidence-based care is not only the humane course of action but also a cost-effective way to retain a ready and healthy military force for the future. By providing one model, the VA is at the forefront of trying to ensure that evidence-based care is delivered to its patient population, but the VA has not yet fully evaluated the success of its efforts across the entire system.

We suggest requiring all providers who treat military personnel to use treatment approaches empirically demonstrated to be effective. This requirement would include uniformed providers in theater and embedded in active duty units; primary and specialty care providers within military health facilities, VA health care facilities, and Vet Centers; and civilian providers. Evidence-based approaches to resilience-building and other programs need to be enforced among informal providers, including promising prevention efforts pre-deployment, models that utilize support from noncommissioned officers in theater, and the work of chaplains and family support providers. Such programs could bolster resilience before mental health conditions develop, or help to mitigate the long-term consequences of mental health conditions.

The goal of this requirement is not to stifle innovation or prevent tailoring treatments to meet individual needs, but to ensure that individuals who have been diagnosed with PTSD or major depression are provided the most effective evidence-based treatment available.

Some key transformations may be required to achieve this needed improvement in the quality of care:

- The "black box" of psychotherapy delivered to veterans must be made more transparent, making providers accountable for the services they are providing. Doing so might require that TRICARE and the VA implement billing codes to indicate the specific type of therapy delivered, documentation requirements (i.e., structured medical note-taking that needs to accompany billing), and the like.
- TRICARE and the VA should require that all patients be treated by therapists who are certified to handle the diagnosed disorders of that patient.
- Veterans should be empowered to seek appropriate care by being informed about what types of therapies to expect, the benefits of such therapies, and how to evaluate for themselves whether they are receiving quality care.
- A monitoring system could be used to ensure sustained quality and coordination of care and quality improvement. Transparency, accountability, and training/certification, as described above, would facilitate ongoing monitoring of effectiveness that could inform policymaking and form the basis for focused quality-improvement initiatives (e.g., through performance measurement and evalua-

tion). Additionally, linking performance measurements to reimbursement and incentives for providers may also promote delivery of quality care.

4.   Invest in research to close information gaps and plan effectively.

In many respects, this study raises more research questions than it provides answers. Better understanding is needed of the full range of problems (emotional, economic, social, health, and other quality-of-life deficits) that confront individuals with post-combat PTSD, major depression, and TBI. This knowledge is required both to enable the health care system to respond effectively and to calibrate how disability benefits are ultimately determined. Greater knowledge is needed to understand who is at risk for developing mental health problems, who is most vulnerable to relapse, and how to target treatments for these individuals.

We need to be able to accurately measure the costs and benefits of different treatment options so that fiscally responsible investments in care can be made. We need to document how these mental health and cognitive conditions affect the families of servicemembers and veterans so that appropriate support services can be provided. We need sustained research into the effectiveness of treatments, particularly treatments that can improve the functioning of individuals who do not improve from the current evidence-based therapies. Finally, we need research that evaluates the effects of policy changes implemented to address the injuries of OEF/OIF veterans, including how such changes affect the health and well-being of the veterans, the costs to society, and the state of military readiness and effectiveness.

Addressing these vital questions will require a substantial, coordinated, and strategic research effort. Further, to adequately address knowledge gaps will require funding mechanisms that encourage longer-term research that examines a broader set of issues than can be financed within the mandated priorities of an existing funder or agency. Such a research program would likely require funding in excess of that currently devoted to PTSD and TBI research through DoD and the VA, and would extend to the National Institutes of Health, the Centers for Disease Control and Prevention, and the Agency for Healthcare Research and Quality. These agencies have limited research activities relevant to military and veteran populations, but these populations have not always been prioritized within their programs.

Initial strategies for implementing this national research agenda include the following:

- Launch a large, longitudinal study on the natural course of these mental health and cognitive conditions among OEF/OIF veterans, including predictors of relapse and recovery. Ideally, such a study would gather data pre-deployment, during deployment, and at multiple time points post-deployment.

The study should be designed so that its findings can be generalized to all deployed servicemembers while still facilitating identification of those at highest risk, and it should focus on the causal associations between deployment and mental health conditions. A longitudinal approach would also make it possible to evaluate how use of health care services affects symptoms, functioning, and outcomes over time; how TBI and mental health conditions affect physical health, economic productivity, and social functioning over the long term; and how these problems affect the spouses and children of servicemembers and veterans. These data would greatly inform how services are arrayed to meet evolving needs within this population of veterans. They would also afford a better understanding of the costs of these conditions and the benefits of treatment so that the nation can make fiscally responsible investments in treatment and prevention programs. Some ongoing studies are examining these issues (Smith et al., 2008; Vasterling et al., 2006). However, they are designed primarily for a different purpose and thus can provide only partial answers.

- Continue to aggressively support research to identify the most effective treatments and approaches, especially for TBI care and rehabilitation. Although many studies are already under way or under review (as a result of the recent congressional mandate for more research on PTSD and TBI), an analysis that identifies priority-research needs within each area could add value to the current programs by informing the overall research agenda and creating new program opportunities in areas in which research may be lacking or needed.
- Evaluate new initiatives, policies, and programs. Many new initiatives and programs designed to address psychological and cognitive injuries have been put into place. Each of these initiatives and programs should be carefully evaluated to ensure that it is effective and is improving over time. Only programs that demonstrate effectiveness should be maintained and disseminated.

Treating the Invisible Wounds of War

Addressing PTSD, depression, and TBI among those who deployed to Afghanistan and Iraq should be a national priority. But it is not an easy undertaking. The prevalence of these injuries is relatively high and may grow as the conflicts continue. And long-term negative consequences are associated with these injuries if they are not treated with evidence-based, patient-centered, efficient, and timely care. The systems of care available to address these injuries have been improved significantly, but critical gaps remain.

The nation must ensure that quality care is available and provided to its military veterans now and in the future. As a group, the veterans returning from Afghanistan and Iraq are predominantly young, healthy, and productive members of society. However, about a third are currently affected by PTSD or depression, or report a possible TBI while deployed. Whether the TBIs will translate into any lasting impairments is unknown. In the absence of knowing, these injuries cause great concern for service-members and their families. These veterans need our attention now to ensure success-ful adjustment post-deployment and full recovery.

Meeting the goal of providing quality care for these servicemembers will require system-level changes, which means expanding our focus to consider issues not just within DoD and the VA, from which the majority of veterans will receive benefits, but across the overall U.S. health care system, where veterans may seek care through other, employer-sponsored health plans and in the public sector (e.g., Medicaid). System-level changes are essential if the nation is to meet not only its need to recruit, prepare, and sustain a military force but also its responsibility to address service-connected injuries and disabilities.

Glossary

active duty	Servicemembers whose military capacity is full-time. Members of the Active Component are considered active duty servicemembers; members of a Reserve Component are not generally considered active duty unless they have been activated, or called up to active duty.
"black box"	A system or process that is viewed primarily in terms of its input and output characteristics, for which the inner workings are not visible, is a *black box*. With regard to psychotherapy, "black box" indicates that what happens in the therapy is usually not observed. The opposite of a black box is a system in which the inner workings are available for inspection.
DoD	The U.S. Department of Defense, the federal department charged with coordinating and supervising all agencies and functions of the government relating directly to national security and the military.
effectiveness	The impact of an intervention on real-world situations.
efficacy	The therapeutic effect of a given intervention, usually evaluated in a clinical trial.
evidence-based care	Certain parts of medical care to which evidence gained from the scientific method has been applied. Such care seeks to assess the quality of evidence relevant to the risks and benefits of treatments (including lack of treatment).

major depression/ depression	*Depression*, or major depressive disorder (MDD), is a mood disorder that interferes with an individual's everyday functioning. Individuals with MDD have a persistent constellation of symptoms, including depressed mood, inability to experience pleasure, or loss of interest in almost all activities, that occur almost every day for two weeks. Other symptoms can include significant weight loss or gain or a decrease in appetite; insomnia or hypersomnia; psychomotor agitation or retardation; fatigue or loss of energy; feelings of worthlessness or excessive or inappropriate guilt; diminished ability to think or concentrate or significant indecisiveness; and recurrent thoughts of death, suicidal ideation, or suicidal attempts or plans. In this monograph, we use the term to indicate MDD or symptoms of this disorder that may not meet full diagnostic criteria.
mental health and cognitive conditions	A *mental health condition* is a problem with mood, thoughts, or behavior that interferes with daily living. In this monograph, we use the term broadly to refer to both diagnosable mental disorders and to symptoms or problems that do not meet the threshold of a diagnosis but nonetheless cause interference in daily living. A *cognitive condition* is a neurological condition that interferes with daily living. In this monograph, we use the term to refer to disruptions in brain function that result from a traumatic brain injury.
mild traumatic brain injury	In contrast to *moderate to severe TBI* (see below), diagnostic criteria for mild TBI include loss of consciousness (for less than 30 minutes), memory loss (for less than 24 hours), and no persistent neurological deficits. For the majority of individuals, symptoms of mild TBI have usually resolved by three months after injury; however, there is a substantial literature indicating that, for some individuals, symptoms may last for 6–12 months or longer. Such individuals may need ongoing medical treatment. The most common physical problems following mild TBI include headache and musculoskeletal pain, disturbance of the vestibular system (which controls eye movements and equilibrium), visual disturbance, and fatigue. Approximately 80 percent of patients with TBIs have mild TBI.

Military OneSource	An information and consultation service offered by the Department of Defense (through the Military, Family, and Community Policy directorate within the Office of the Under Secretary of Defense for Personnel & Readiness) to servicemembers in the Active and Reserve Components (regardless of activation status) and their families. Retired or separated servicemembers and their family members are eligible to receive services at no cost for up to six months after separation.
minimally adequate care	The number and duration of treatments, not whether an individual was documented to have received an effective intervention. Participants were judged to have had a *minimally adequate trial of a psychoactive drug* if they (1) had taken a prescribed medication as long as the doctor wanted and (2) had at least 4 visits with a doctor or therapist in the past 12 months. *Minimally adequate exposure to psychotherapy* was defined as having had at least 8 visits with a "mental health professional such as a psychiatrist, psychologist or counselor" in the past 12 months, with visits averaging at least 30 minutes. Criteria for *minimally adequate courses of treatment* were adapted from the National Comorbidity Study Replication (Wang et al., 2005).
moderate to severe TBI	A head injury that results in loss of consciousness (more than 30 minutes), memory loss (more than 24 hours), and persistent neurological deficits. In general, the problems last longer and are more severe than in mild TBI, and they generally require rehabilitation services. See *mild traumatic brain injury* (above).
morbidity	A measure of the rate of sickness in a given population.
mortality	A measure of the number of deaths in a given population.
MTF	Military Treatment Facility; DoD-owned facilities that provide health care support services.
OEF	Operation Enduring Freedom, the military operation that began in 2001 in Afghanistan
OIF	Operation Iraqi Freedom, the military operation in Iraq. Although troop buildup began in 2002, the invasion of Iraq occurred in March 2003.

patient-centered care	Care in which the values and preferences of individuals are respected in clinical decisionmaking and the patients are fully informed participants in decisions about their treatment. Principles of patient-centered care also suggest that, to improve quality of care, it will be important to orient care around each specific patient's preferences and needs.
post-stratification weights	Values that can be used to improve the representativeness of the analytic sample relative to the target population and to account for nonresponse in the sampling. Here, we used them to adjust the data we collected to make the analyses representative of the target population (all those deployed to OEF/OIF): To match the target population on the branch of Service and within each branch of Service, it is weighted to balance on median age, gender, marital status, officer rank, currently separated duty status, and Reserve Component. The characteristics of the population of previously deployed servicemembers were derived from the Contingency Tracking System Deployment File and the Work Experiences File from the Defense Manpower Data Center (DMDC).
post-traumatic stress disorder, or PTSD	An anxiety disorder that occurs after a traumatic event in which a threat of serious injury or death was experienced or witnessed and to which the individual responds with intense fear, helplessness, or horror. In addition, the disorder is marked by the following symptoms occurring for more than one month and causing significant distress and/or impairment: re-experiencing the event, avoiding stimuli relating to the event, numbing of general responsiveness, and hyperarousal (American Psychiatric Association, 2000). PTSD is diagnosed only after symptoms have persisted for more than 30 days after exposure to a traumatic event.
productivity	The rate at which an individual produces goods and services having a market exchange value, either in a place of business or a home.

Reserve Components	Military organizations with members who generally perform a minimum of 39 days of military duty per year and who augment the active duty (or full-time) military when necessary. They include the Army Reserves, Army National Guard, Navy Reserves, Air National Guard, Air Force Reserve, Coast Guard Reserve, and the Marine Corps Reserves, which are also referred to collectively as "the Guard and Reserves." In this monograph, we use the term *Reserve Component servicemembers* to include reservists and guardsmen.
sensitivity	The *validity* of a screening tool can be measured by its *sensitivity*, or the proportion of persons with a given condition correctly identified by the screening tool as having the condition, and its *specificity*, or the proportion of persons without a condition correctly identified by the screening tool as not having the disorder.
service-connected	Injuries or other illnesses that are related, a function of, or otherwise connected to military service. In this monograph, it relates to eligibility for post-discharge benefits from the DoD and the VA.
servicemembers	Members of the military services in both the Active and Reserve Components.
societal costs	All costs that accrue to any member of U.S. society, including the government, military servicemembers, their families, taxpayers, employers, and others.
statistical life	A hypothetical individual who might be saved by a particular intervention or policy change, as opposed to an actual person, termed an *identified life*. In economics, a means of calculating the value of a lost life. The value of an identified life would far exceed that of a statistical life and cannot be appropriately quantified using economic techniques.
suicide costs	Health care costs for suicide attempts and completions (e.g., emergency room visits, hospitalizations) and the value of lives lost to suicide. The value of a life lost to suicide uses published estimates of the *value of a statistical life* (see above), including differences across occupations in wage and risk-of-dying, to estimate an approximate value of life for a statistical individual. In theory, these estimates should capture all costs associated with death that would conceivably be valued by a worker, including lost quality of life, grief and loss to family members, and pain and suffering.

traumatic brain injury, or TBI	An injury to the brain, whether or not it is associated with lasting functional impairment. The exact nature of the symptoms depends upon the type and severity of the injury. Injuries include penetrating injuries, closed head injuries, and exposure to blasts. Disruptions in brain functioning can include a decreased level of consciousness, amnesia, or other neurological or neuropsychological abnormalities.
TRICARE	The health plan of the Military Health System. Roughly 9 million active duty servicemembers, active duty family members, retirees, and families of retirees are eligible to receive medical care through TRICARE.
VA	The U.S. Department of Veterans Affairs, which provides patient care and federal benefits to military veterans.
Vet Centers	Affiliated with the Department of Veterans Affairs and often located in storefront settings, Vet Centers offer individual and group counseling, marital and family counseling, bereavement counseling for family members, medical referrals, assistance in applying for VA benefits, employment counseling, military sexual-trauma counseling, alcohol and drug assessments, outreach, and community education. Services are offered at no cost to eligible veterans and their families, and there is no limit on the duration or frequency of services. Any veteran who has served in a war zone is eligible for care at a Vet Center.
veteran	A former member of the armed forces or someone who served in major combat operations: However, whether an individual is considered a *veteran* may depend on which veteran's benefit or service program the person is applying for, because eligibility criteria for each program (burial/cemetery, health care, disability, etc.) varies by program. In this monograph, *OEF/OIF veteran* includes all military servicemembers who served in Operations Enduring Freedom and/or Iraqi Freedom.

References

Altmire, Jason. *Testimony of Jason Altmire*, Hearing Before the Subcommittee on Health of the House Committee on Veterans' Affairs, Washington, D.C., 2007.

American Psychiatric Association. *Diagnostic and Statistical Manual*, Version Four. Washington, D.C., 2000.

American Psychological Association (APA). Practice guideline for the treatment of patients with major depressive disorder (revision). *American Journal of Psychiatry,* Vol. 157, No. 4, Suppl., April 2000, pp. 1-45.

Armed Forces Health Surveillance. *Medical Surveillance Monthly Report.* As of January 17, 2008: http://amsa.army.mil/1msmr/MSMR_TOC.htm

Belasco, A. *The Cost of Iraq, Afghanistan, and Other Global War on Terror Operations Since 9/11.* Washington, D.C.: Congressional Research Service, 2007.

Bruner, E. F. *Military Forces: What Is the Appropriate Size for the United States?* Washington, D.C.: Congressional Research Service, 2006.

Centers for Disease Control and Prevention, National Center for Injury Prevention and Control Web site, Traumatic Brain Injury page, 2008. As of January 25, 2008: http://www.cdc.gov/ncipc/factsheets/tbi.htm

Dean, E. T., Jr. *Shook Over Hell—Post-Traumatic Stress, Vietnam, and the Civil War.* Cambridge, Mass.: Harvard University Press, 1997.

Defense and Veterans Brain Injury Center. "Informational Brochure" unpublished, 2005.

Department of Defense (DoD) Personnel and Procurement Statistics Web site, Military Casualty Information page. As of December 8, 2007: http://siadapp.dmdc.osd.mil/personnel/CASUALTY/castop.htm

Department of Defense Task Force on Mental Health. *An Achievable Vision: Report of the Department of Defense Task Force on Mental Health.* Falls Church, Va.: Defense Health Board, June 2007.

Department of Veterans Affairs, Office of Policy, Planning, and Preparedness. *Evaluation of Services for Seriously Mentally Ill Patients in the Veterans Health Administration of the Department of Veterans Affairs: Revised Statement of Work.* Washington, D.C., March 2006.

Department of Veterans Affairs Web site, Health Care—Veterans Health Administration page. As of July 2007:
http://www1.va.gov/health/gateway.html

"Executive Order Establishing Task Force; Executive Order 13426—Establishing a Commission on Care for America's Returning Wounded Warriors and a Task Force on Returning Global War on Terror Heroes." *Federal Register,* March 8, 2007, Appendix A. As of December 31, 2007: http://www1.va.gov/taskforce/

Friedman, M. J. Acknowledging the psychiatric cost of war. *New England Journal of Medicine,* Vol. 351, No. 1, July 1, 2004, pp. 75–77.

————, Posttraumatic stress disorder among military returnees from Afghanistan and Iraq. *The American Journal of Psychiatry,* Vol. 163, No. 4, April 2006, pp. 586–593.

Glasser, R. A shock wave of brain injuries. *The Washington Post,* April 8, 2007. As of February 22, 2008: http://www.washingtonpost.com/wp-dyn/content/article/2007/04/06/AR2007040601821.html

Government Accountability Office (GAO). *Posttraumatic Stress Disorder: DoD Needs to Identify the Factors Its Providers Use to Make Mental Health Evaluation Referrals for Service Members.* Washington, D.C., 2006.

Helmus, T. C., and R. W. Glenn. *Steeling the Mind: Combat Stress Reactions and Their Implications for Urban Warfare.* Santa Monica, Calif.: RAND Corporation, MG-191-A, 2005. http://www.rand.org/pubs/monographs/MG191/

Hoge, C. W., S. E. Lesikar, R. Guevara, J. Lange, J. F. Brundage, Jr., C. C. Engel, S. C. Messer, and D. T. Orman. Mental disorders among U.S. military personnel in the 1990s: Association with high levels of health care utilization and early military attrition. *American Journal of Psychiatry,* Vol. 159, No. 9, September 2002, pp. 1576–1583.

Hoge, C. W., C. A. Castro, S. C. Messer, D. McGurk, D. I. Cotting, and R. L. Koffman. Combat duty in Iraq and Afghanistan, mental health problems, and barriers to care. *New England Journal of Medicine,* Vol. 351, No. 1, July 2004, pp. 13–22.

Hoge, C. W., J. L. Auchterlonie, and C. S. Milliken. Mental health problems, use of mental health services, and attrition from military service after returning from deployment to Iraq or Afghanistan. *JAMA,* Vol. 295, No. 9, March 1, 2006, pp. 1023–1032.

Hoge, C. W., A. Terhakopian, C. A. Castro, S. C. Messer, and C. C. Engel. Association of posttraumatic stress disorder with somatic symptoms, health care visits, and absenteeism among Iraq War veterans. *American Journal of Psychiatry,* Vol. 164, No. 1, January 2007, pp. 150–153. As of January 23, 2008: http://www.ncbi.nlm.nih.gov/entrez/query.fcgi?cmd=Retrieve&db=PubMed&dopt=Citation&list_uids=17202557

Hoge, C. W., D. McGurk, J. L. Thomas, A. L Cox, C. C Engel, and C. A. Castro. Mild traumatic brain injury in U.S. soldiers returning from Iraq. *New England Journal of Medicine,* Vol. 358, No. 5, January 31, 2008, pp. 453–463.

Hosek, J., J. Kavanagh, and L. Miller. *How Deployments Affect Service Members.* Santa Monica, Calif.: RAND Corporation, MG-432-RC, 2006.

Independent Review Group. *Rebuilding the Trust.* Washington, D.C., 2007.

Institute of Medicine. *Crossing the Quality Chasm: A New Health System for the 21st Century.* Washington, DC: National Academies Press, 2001.

Institute of Medicine, Committee on Crossing the Quality Chasm: Adaptation to Mental Health and Addictive Disorders. *Improving the Quality of Health Care for Mental and Substance-Use Conditions: Quality Chasm Series.* Washington, D.C.: National Academies Press, 2006.

Institute of Medicine, Committee on Monitoring Access to Personal Health Care Services. *Access to Health Care in America*. Washington, D.C.: National Academies Press, 1993.

Institute of Medicine, Committee on Treatment of Posttraumatic Stress Disorder, Board on Population Health and Public Health Practice. *Treatment of Posttraumatic Stress Disorder: An Assessment of the Evidence*. Washington, D.C.: National Academies Press, 2007.

Jones, E., and I. P. Palmer. Army psychiatry in the Korean War: The experience of 1 Commonwealth Division. *Military Medicine,* Vol. 165, No. 4, April 2000, pp. 256–260.

Marlowe, D. H. *Psychological and Psychosocial Consequences of Combat and Deployment, with Special Emphasis on the Gulf War*. Santa Monica, Calif: RAND Corporation, MR-1018/11-OSD, 2001. As of February 22, 2008:
http://www.rand.org/pubs/monograph_reports/MR1018.11/

Milliken, C. S., J. L. Auchterlonie, and C. W. Hoge. Longitudinal assessment of mental health problems among Active and Reserve Component soldiers returning from the Iraq War. *JAMA,* Vol. 298, No. 18, 2007, pp. 2141–2148.

National Center for Biotechnology Information. PubMed database. As of August 2007:
http://www.pubmed.gov

National Governors Association Web site. As of January 17, 2008:
http://www.nga.org/

National Institute of Mental Health Web site, Mental Health Topics page. As of February 11, 2008:
http://www.nimh.nih.gov/health/topics/index.shtml

National Institute of Neurological Disorders and Stroke (U.S.). *Traumatic Brain Injury: Hope Through Research*. Bethesda, Md., NIH Publication No. 02-158, 2002. As of January 30, 2008:
http://www.ninds.nih.gov/disorders/tbi/detail%5Ftbi.htm

Newman, R. A. Combat fatigue: A review of the Korean Conflict. *Military Medicine,* Vol. 129, 1964, pp. 921–928.

President's Commission on Care for America's Returning Wounded Warriors. *Serve, Support, Simplify: Report of the President's Commission on Care for America's Returning Wounded Warriors*. Washington, D.C., July 2007. As of January 23, 2008:
http://www.pccww.gov/index.html

Regan, T. Report: High survival rate for US troops wounded in Iraq. *Christian Science Monitor,* November 29, 2004.

Rosenheck, R. Changing patterns of care for war-related post-traumatic stress disorder at Department of Veterans Affairs Medical Centers: The use of performance data to guide program development. *Military Medicine,* Vol. 164, No. 11, November 1999, pp. 795–802.

Serafino, N. M. *Peacekeeping: Issues of U.S. Military Involvement*. Washington, D.C.: Congressional Research Service, 2003.

Smith, T. C., M. A. K. Ryan, D. L. Wingard, D. J. Slymen, J. F. Sallis, and D. Kritz-Silverstein. New onset and persistent symptoms of post-traumatic stress disorder self reported after deployment and combat exposures: Prospective population based US military cohort study. *British Medical Journal.* January 15, 2008: Published online.

Tanielian, T., and L. Jaycox (Eds.). *Invisible Wounds of War: Psychological and Cognitive Injuries, Their Consequences, and Services to Assist Recovery*. Santa Monica, Calif.: RAND Corporation, MG-720-CCF, 2008.

Thurman, D. J., J. E. Sniezek, D. Johnson, A. Greenspan, and S. M. Smith. *Guidelines for Surveillance of Central Nervous System Injury.* Atlanta, Ga.: Centers for Disease Control and Prevention, 1995.

Vasterling, J. J., S. P. Proctor, P. Amoroso, R. Kane, T. Heeren, and R. F. White. Neuropsychological outcomes of Army personnel following deployment to the Iraq War. *JAMA,* Vol. 296, No. 5, August 2, 2006, pp. 519–529. http://www.ncbi.nlm.nih.gov/entrez/query.fcgi?cmd=Retrieve&db=PubMed&dopt= Citation&list_uids=16882958

Wang, P. S., M. Lane, M. Olfson, H. A. Pincus, K. Wells, and K. C. Kessler. Twelve-month use of mental health services in the United States: Results from the National Comorbidity Survey Replication. *Archives of General Psychiatry,* Vol. 62, 2005, pp. 629–640.

Warden, D. Military TBI during the Iraq and Afghanistan Wars. *Journal of Head Trauma Rehabilitation,* Vol. 21, No. 5, 2006, pp. 398–402.